THE
CHEAP, FAST & EASY
COOKBOOK

THE
CHEAP, FAST & EASY
COOKBOOK

Roadside Amusements
Published by Chamberlain Bros.
a member of
Penguin Group (USA) Inc.
New York
2005

Roadside Amusements

Published by the Penguin Group

Penguin Group (USA) Inc., 375 Hudson Street, New York, New York 10014, USA

Penguin Group (Canada), 10 Alcorn Avenue, Toronto, Ontario M4V 3B2, Canada (a division of Pearson Penguin Canada Inc.)

Penguin Books Ltd, 80 Strand, London WC2R 0RL, England

Penguin Ireland, 25 St Stephen's Green, Dublin 2, Ireland (a division of Penguin Books Ltd)

Penguin Group (Australia), 250 Camberwell Road, Camberwell, Victoria 3124, Australia (a division of Pearson Australia Group Pty Ltd)

Penguin Books India Pvt Ltd, 11 Community Centre, Panchsheel Park, New Delhi—110 017, India

Penguin Group (NZ), Cnr Airborne and Rosedale Roads, Albany, Auckland 1310, New Zealand (a division of Pearson New Zealand Ltd)

Penguin Books (South Africa) (Pty) Ltd, 24 Sturdee Avenue, Rosebank, Johannesburg 2196, South Africa

Penguin Books Ltd, Registered Offices: 80 Strand, London WC2R 0RL, England

Copyright © 2005 by Chamberlain Bros.

Published simultaneously in Canada

An application has been submitted to register this book with the Library of Congress.

Printed in the United States of America

1 3 5 7 9 10 8 6 4 2

Book design by Scribe, Inc. (www.scribenet.com)

PUBLISHER'S NOTE

The recipes contained in this book are to be followed exactly as written. The Publisher is not responsible for your specific health or allergy needs that may require medical supervision. The Publisher is not responsible for any adverse reactions to the recipes contained in this book.

CONTENTS

Acknowledgments   vii

Introduction   ix

Chapter 1: Breakfast   1

Chapter 2: Lunch   15

Chapter 3: Dinner   31

Chapter 4: Snacks and Study Breaks   51

Chapter 5: Party Food   65

Chapter 6: Dessert   79

Chapter 7: Beverages   93

Chapter 8: Holiday Meals and Special Occasions   105

Chapter 9: Off-Campus Cooking   121

About the DVD   143

ACKNOWLEDGMENTS

This book would not have been possible without the efforts of several key contributors, especially Pamela Liflander and Raisa Grinshpun. Additional thanks and credit to David Rech, Mark Fretz, Andy Brown, and Brandon Smith at Scribe, as well as to Mike Rivilis, the editor, Ron Martirano, and the publisher, Carlo De Vito.

Special thanks to everyone at The Rutgers University Television Network, especially Christopher Waters, Matthew Weismantel, Lisa Hope King, Jaimini Shah, Alex Fahan, and the entire cast and crew of the Cheap Fast & Easy Cooking video production team.

Also, thank you to the Association of Higher Education Cable Television Administrators (AHECTA) member institutions for distributing this series to resident students.

Finally, our heartfelt gratitude to the Cheap, Fast & Easy house band, Yardsdale, whose latest CD can be picked up at www.yardsdale.com.

INTRODUCTION

Even if you are on a perfect meal plan that serves up three hot meals a day in a stunning environment with great-looking waiters and waitresses, white linens, and fresh flowers on every table, there will be meals you will miss. Maybe your cafeteria isn't this glamorous. Maybe the food is inedible. Maybe you overslept...again, and missed dinner.

Whatever the reason, this book provides the solution. Inside you'll find over one hundred recipes you can prepare that are cheap, fast, & easy. They are foods you are familiar with and love, although there may be a few surprises and different twists on your favorites. Most recipes contain no more than five ingredients, so there's not a lot of shopping to do. Many rely heavily on stuff you already love, like ramen noodles, mac and cheese, and cold cereal. Best, each recipe takes just a few minutes to prepare, and most can be made and consumed within a half hour (most will be much less!). So whether you've missed breakfast, lunch, or dinner, we've got you covered. If you're throwing your first dorm-room party, no sweat. And if you are trying to impress someone special with your culinary talents, we've supplied everything you need to know about creating a romantic dinner. What's more, when you finally leave the dorm, there's a whole bunch of recipes for when you can get your hands on a real oven. By that time, you'll be ready for your own show on the Food Network!

Start Shopping

All the recipes in this book can be made without a traditional oven, and use appliances that don't take up much room. You'll need access to what we like to call "the big six," although a few are more important than others:

- mini-fridge: must have, many rooms come with one
- small kitchen-size electric grill: must have
- microwave oven: must have, and you'll soon realize why it's more important to you than your friends
- blender: you'll really want this, but only applies to a handful of recipes
- hot pot: if you have a microwave oven you can live without this, but it does come in handy
- coffeemaker: if you like to save money on your fresh-brewed coffee we suggest that you swing for this. Otherwise, you can survive on instant coffee (which you can make in the microwave oven) and splurge on the hot java when you leave your room.

If you're lucky enough to read this before you leave home, you can save lots of money by asking your family to donate some of these small kitchen appliances. You may want to coordinate purchasing these with your roommates as well. At worst, shop while your parents are still on campus and provide access to their credit cards. If they've left town, get on the Internet and order, either new or used, but make sure that they are clean and have some sort of warranty. Most of these appliances, even the best models, won't last through your entire college career.

Not All Appliances Are Created Equal

All electric appliances, including microwave ovens, blenders, and especially electric grills, are made slightly differently from one another. Some are bigger than others, and some are actually more powerful. Carefully read the instructions that come in the box before using them. For example, note the time it takes for an electric grill to warm up and the directions on how to use it. You'll have to experiment with each of these appliances before you do important cooking, especially if you are cooking a special meal or preparing food for others.

Smaller-Ticket Items

Aside from the big six, there are a few kitchen items you can't live without. While most of these won't take up much space (you can fit them all in one milk crate), the cost of these will quickly add up. See if you can split up this list with others around you: just remember who owns what. However you decide the finances, you'll definitely need the following:

- microwavable plastic wrap
- microwavable utensils
- microwavable bowl(s) (we suggest three of different sizes, see if you can get the ones with lids)
- microwavable mug(s)
- paper towels
- dishwashing liquid
- a few sponges
- measuring cup
- measuring spoons
- can opener
- cutting board and knife
- zip-top plastic bags
- whisk

- wooden spoon
- spatula
- saucer or small plate
- garbage pail

Stocking a Pantry: Goods You'll Use More Than Once

Good cooks try to have in stock the ingredients they need. Set aside one drawer in the room, even if it,s a desk drawer, to store nonperishable goods. Choose your favorites from this list, and make sure to have at least three or four of each on hand. Read labels carefully, and see what needs to be refrigerated after opening. When it comes to the spices, buy one of each: they should last at least through your first term.

- cans of chicken, tuna, or ham
- ramen noodles and instant soups
- canned veggies, such as corn, peas, and green beans
- dry breakfast cereal
- dried fruits (raisins, apricots, cranberries)
- peanut butter
- jam
- granola bars
- sweetened condensed milk
- individual containers of unrefrigerated, boxed milk (which has a long shelf life)
- pasta sauce
- salsa
- salad dressing
- mac and cheese
- microwave rice (brown/white)
- olive oil
- white vinegar (any variety, like white balsamic, cider, or regular distilled)
- dried herbs and spices, including cinnamon, oregano, cilantro, parsley, salt, pepper, and nutmeg

Keeping Your Fridge Happy

Your refrigerator is going to be small, so it is best to rely on it only for storing foods once they are opened. There are two types of food that can go in the fridge: the kind that eventually spoils and the kind that doesn't. Here's the list:

- **FOODS THAT KEEP FOREVER:** butter, American cheese singles, lemon juice.
- **FOODS THAT WILL SPOIL, GO MOLDY, OR STALE:** Everything else, including eggs (2 weeks tops), milk, or anything made with milk including real cheese, cream cheese, and yogurt (once opened), and fruit and veggies (which also have about a 2-week shelf life).

What's in Your Cafeteria?

Should you run out of ingredients, you can always borrow from friends or neighbors. Many of the recipes in this book can be made with little more than the ingredients you can find for free in the cafeteria, your local deli, fast-food hangout, Asian takeout, or coffeehouse. Don't throw away those extra condiment packets you got with your lunch, see on the table, or in those big metal bins. Instead, bring them back to your room and "recycle." Scout out and stock up on the following (but be discreet):

- ketchup, mustard, and mayonnaise
- salt and pepper
- soup crackers or saltines
- salad dressing
- salsa
- maple syrup
- honey
- butter or margarine pats
- tea bags
- coffee creamer
- napkins
- plastic utensils

- straws
- paper cups
- toothpicks

Ask ahead if you can take real food out of the cafeteria. If you're allowed, you'll be amazed at what might be there. If your cafeteria has a dessert bar or salad bar, look for items with a long shelf life. These will not be packaged, but you might be able to carry out a small amount at a time (stick to no more than a handful).

- raisins, or other dried fruits
- chocolate chips
- nuts
- coconut shavings
- fresh whole fruits like apples, bananas, or oranges

Not All Packets Are Created Equal, Either

Through our tireless research we have come to learn that not all takeout packets of condiments contain the same amounts of ingredients. For instance, most soy sauce from Asian takeout yields about a tablespoon, but some are so skimpy that they yield only a teaspoon. That's a big difference, because it takes 3 teaspoons to equal 1 tablespoon. Your best bet when relying on freebies is to make sure you have a few extras on hand, and then pour the contents of the packets into a measuring spoon before adding to your recipe. That way, you'll know you have the right amount.

BREAKFAST

Breakfast is the most important meal of the day, and when you make it yourself, your day will be off to a good start. What's more, you'll save yourself a bundle by eating in and brewing your own coffee.

Basic Omelet

Equipment Needed: microwave oven, bowl, microwavable plate, plastic wrap

Preparation Time: 3 minutes

Ingredients:

> 2 eggs
> 1 teaspoon milk, or 1 tiny takeout packet coffee creamer
> 1 tablespoon water
> 1 teaspoon butter (½ pat)

Preparation:

1. Mix eggs together with milk and water, and set aside.
2. Butter a microwavable plate.
3. Pour egg mixture on the plate, and cover tightly with plastic wrap. Microwave on HIGH for 1½ to 2 minutes. When cooked, the center of the omelet may still be moist.

Servings: 1

Go-Crazy Add-ons:

Basically, you can get rid of anything in your fridge to make this a heartier breakfast. Before you cook the eggs, see what you have left over. You can use up to 2 to 3 tablespoons of any leftover vegetables—like tomatoes, peppers, or onions—by placing them on top of the eggs, inside the plastic wrap, before you cook them. Throw in a tablespoon or two of any canned vegetable. Cheese can be added before or after the cooking process. If you want it melted into the eggs, make sure to break it up into little pieces. Think outside of the American cheese single, and try a slice of Cheddar, Muenster, or Swiss, or really go crazy and add crumbled feta cheese.

The Morning-After Mexican Eggs

If last night was a little more than you bargained for, here's a hearty breakfast to get you back on track. Two Tylenol pills and a big glass of water aren't a bad idea, either.

Equipment Needed: microwave oven, two microwavable bowls, plastic wrap

Preparation Time: 2 minutes

Ingredients:

> 2 eggs
> 2 tablespoons water
> 1 teaspoon butter (½ pat)
> 1 handful tortilla chips
> 2 tablespoons salsa

Preparation:

1. Mix together eggs and water in a bowl. Set aside.
2. Coat the second bowl with butter and pour in egg mixture. Cover tightly with plastic wrap.
3. Place bowl in the microwave oven. Microwave on HIGH for 1½ to 2 minutes. During the cooking process the eggs will rise and fall. When done, the center of the omelet may still be moist. That's OK.
4. Meanwhile, arrange a plate with tortilla chips. Transfer the omelet onto the plate, placing the eggs on top of the chips. Drizzle the salsa over the eggs.

Servings: 1

Poached Eggs and Breakfast Sausages

For the really big breakfast, nothing beats the morning trifecta of eggs, bread, and breakfast meat.

Equipment Needed: electric grill, microwave oven, microwavable, small deep bowl

Preparation Time: 10 minutes

Ingredients:

> ½ cup water
> 2 eggs
> 4 precooked breakfast sausage links
> 1 slice bread

Preparation:

1. Preheat grill as directed.
2. Pour the ½ cup of water into a microwavable bowl. Break the eggs directly into the bowl without breaking the yolks. Carefully prick the membrane covering each yolk with a knife tip or toothpick, but without piercing the yolk. This will ensure that the egg will not explode during the cooking process.
3. Cover the bowl with plastic wrap. Place bowl in microwave oven, and microwave on HIGH for 1½ to 2 minutes. Use the steam created inside the plastic wrap to completely cook the eggs. Don't uncover the bowl until the egg whites are set and yolks begin to thicken but are not hard (an additional 1 to 2 minutes).
4. Meanwhile, put the breakfast sausages on the preheated grill and cook as directed. Take sausages off the grill, and place the bread on the grill to heat up, no more than 1 minute.
5. When you are ready, transfer the eggs, sausages, and bread onto a clean plate.

Servings: 1

Go-Crazy Swaps:

Swap out the sausage for your favorite breakfast meat. Use the electric grill for heating up Canadian bacon, sausage patties, vegetable patties, or slices of Spam. Use your microwave to sizzle up a side of bacon. If you don't like poached eggs, swap for another cooking method: you can make scrambled eggs/omelet from the earlier eggs recipes, or boil two eggs in your hot pot (that one will take a while).

Save the Packs!

Invariably, after a run to your favorite fast-food establishment, or the one that's open latest, your car or room is dotted with unused takeout condiment packets. Save them! Store them in a dry, dark, cool place. They will keep for some time, and they can come in quite handy! Whether it's chicken tonight, or salads, Italian, Chinese, Mexican, or diner food, here are some essentials to look out for. They're like cereal-box prizes, only without the choking hazard (mostly).

- Chicken (nuggets, wings, fried): Sauces (BBQ, sweet-and-sour, honey mustard), dressings (bleu cheese, ranch)
- Chinese: Sauces (soy, hot mustard, duck, hot), noodles
- Italian: Parmesan cheese
- Salads: Dressings, bacon bits, croutons, cheese
- Mexican: Picante sauce, sour cream
- Breakfast: Takeout packets (sugar, jelly, honey, cream cheese)

> ### Cooking Bacon in a Microwave Oven
>
> You can buy racks to sling bacon slabs over for microwaving, but we've found that it is just as easy to make bacon on a regular, microwavable plate. Just take 3 to 4 strips of bacon and place on a microwavable plate lined with two sheets of paper towel. Microwave on HIGH for 3 minutes. If the bacon is not crispy, cook for an additional 30 seconds. Repeat in 30-second increments until crispy. Immediately remove from the paper towel and place on a clean plate. Otherwise, the paper towels will stick to the bacon. Use more clean paper towels to wipe down the microwave oven when you're done.

Cinnamon French Toast

Equipment Needed: electric grill, bowl, fork or spoon

Preparation Time: 5 minutes

Ingredients:

> 1 egg
> 2 tablespoons water
> 1 teaspoon ground cinnamon
> 1 slice white bread (preferably day old)
> 1 tablespoon sugar (3 takeout packets)

Preparation:

1. Preheat electric grill as directed.
2. Beat the egg in a bowl large enough to fit a slice of bread. Add the water and mix. Then, add the cinnamon. Because

cinnamon may not mix well with cold liquids, you may find it easier to sprinkle in the cinnamon as you mix it.

3. Place the bread into the liquid and soak on each side for about 1 minute.
4. Carefully transfer the bread onto the preheated grill. If any egg mixture remains in the bowl, don't waste it! Pour it slowly over the bread. Cook for 1 to 2 minutes.
5. After removing the toast, sprinkle it with sugar.

Servings: 1

Hot Oatmeal Upgrades

Fortunately, you can now find individual packages of oatmeal that are much better than the presweetened mush you had to eat as a kid.

FRUITS	NUTS/SEEDS
1 banana, or ½ cup dried	2 ounces crushed walnuts
3 ounces dried papaya	2 ounces unsalted, shelled sunflower seeds
3 ounces dried cranberries	2 ounces almond slivers

These recipes require you to stock up on dried fruits and nuts, so check out the offerings at the dessert bar in the cafeteria, and ask if you can take a cup (or two) to go. If you can get to the supermarket, fresh varieties are always better.

Equipment Needed: Hot pot or microwave oven, spoon, microwavable bowl and lid or plastic wrap

Preparation Time: 5 minutes

Ingredients:

1 (1-serving) package unsweetened oatmeal, or ⅔ cup if you buy in bulk

1.5 teaspoons honey (1 takeout packet)
1 teaspoon butter (½ pat)
2 tablespoons any of the upgrade ingredients listed above
Water per packaged instructions (you can usually substitute the same quantity of milk if you have any)

Preparation:

Prepare the oatmeal according to the package instructions. Add the honey and butter and any add-ons, and mix. Let stand for 1 or 2 minutes before eating.

Servings: 1

Fruit-Found-in-the-Cafeteria Smoothie

Equipment Needed: blender

Preparation Time: 3 minutes

Ingredients:

1 (6–8 ounce) cup yogurt, any flavor
1 ripe banana, peeled

Preparation:

Put the yogurt and banana into a blender and mix until the drink gets to a consistency of a smoothie.

Servings: 1

Go-Crazy Swaps:

You can add ½ cup strawberries, blueberries, or raspberries. If your yogurt is not sweetened with fruit you can add two takeout packets sugar. Or for something really exotic, try swapping the banana for 1 cup papaya, peeled and cut into 1-inch squares. If you don't have a blender, just peel and cut any of these fruits into smaller, bite-size pieces, mix in your yogurt, and eat right out of the container.

Breakfast Yogurt with a Granola Spoon

We stumbled on this breakfast treat out of desperation and a mountain of unwashed dishes.

Equipment Needed: none

Preparation Time: 0

Ingredients:

>   1 (6–8 ounce) cup yogurt, any flavor
>   1 granola bar

Preparation:

1. Open the yogurt container. Use the granola bar as a spoon by dunking it into yogurt each time you bite.
2. Eat granola bar during or after.

Servings: 1

Cereal Matrix

Equipment Needed: bowl, spoon

Preparation Time: nil

A cereal bar is now more than a prepackaged breakfast treat. Popping up near college campuses are entire establishments that exclusively sell dry cereal and milk, mixing them any way you like. Why bother going to them? You can do the same thing without leaving the dorm. Just make sure to buy fresh milk.

A great cereal pantry consists of base cereals, specialty sweetened cereals, dried or fresh fruits, and baking items like chocolate chips, marshmallows, or unsalted nuts. The first step is to create a base: pour 1 cup of the cereal product into a bowl. You don't have to limit yourself to one kind of cereal at a time: mix and match as you see fit. Then, use the following matrix for topping ideas to make the old morning routine of cereal and milk that much more interesting, without taking up any more of your time.

BASE CEREAL (1 CUP)	DRIED FRUIT (1 HEAPING TABLESPOON)	DRIED NUTS/ SEEDS/CHIPS (1 HEAPING TABLESPOON)	FRESH FRUIT
Cornflakes cereal	Raisins	Walnuts	½ banana, sliced
Chocolaty cereal	Dried cranberries	Sliced almonds	½cup blueberries
Fruity cereal	Strawberries	Crushed cashews	4 strawberries, sliced
Oat bran cereal	Bananas	Chocolate chips	½ apple, sliced
High-fiber cereal	Papaya	Sunflower seeds	½ small papaya, peeled and sliced
O's of any flavor	Prunes, sliced or "breakfast size"	Pumpkin seeds	½ mango, peeled and sliced

Crazy New Idea for Cereal Addicts

It wasn't until we went to Germany one spring break that we realized that Americans are entirely missing the boat on cereal. We always thought cereal went with milk, but it really tastes much better when mixed with yogurt! Next time, transfer your yogurt into a bowl. Pour on your favorite cereal or granola mix. Eat with a real spoon.

Fruit Breakfast Basket

Equipment Needed: knife and spoon

Preparation Time: 1 minute

Ingredients:

　　　½ cantaloupe, seeds scooped out
　　　½ cup cottage cheese

1 tablespoon raisins or other dried fruit (cranberries, dried figs, prunes, apricots)
1 tablespoon nuts (walnuts, pecans, or almonds)

Preparation:

1. Place the cottage cheese inside the cantaloupe hollow.
2. Sprinkle with the remaining ingredients.

Servings: 1

New York Breakfast—Home-Cured Salmon (with bagels and cream cheese)

When you first look at this recipe, you'll be thinking, this doesn't look cheap, fast, or easy. But it is really all three! This is a recipe that will not only impress yourself, but it will impress your friends. Making your own lox costs a fraction of the price of store-bought, it lasts forever, and tastes infinitely fresher. So don't be scared: give it a try!

Equipment Needed: nonreactive (glass, ceramic, or stainless steel) baking dish at least 4 inches deep and long enough to hold the salmon, sharp knife, plastic wrap, and your biology (economics, psychology, whatever) textbooks

Preparation Time: 5 minutes one day before; 15 minutes the day of serving

Ingredients:

1 (1-pound) box kosher salt
1 pound salmon fillet, skin on but bones removed, rinsed and patted dry
4 teaspoons sugar (4 takeout packets)
4 bagels

1 (8-ounce) tub cream cheese (buy the biggest regular size, since it keeps well in the fridge)

Preparation:

1. Cover the bottom of a baking dish completely with a layer of kosher salt.
2. Put the salmon fillet skin side down into the salt bed and pour more kosher salt over the fish. Pour enough salt so that it completely covers the sides and the top of the fish. In total, it is very possible that you will use more than half of the box.
3. Sprinkle the top of the fish with the sugar, mixing it with the salt.
4. Cover the dish tightly with plastic wrap and then weight down the wrap with at least 10 pounds. Use your textbooks as weights. You want to make sure that the books are pressing directly onto the wrap that is pressing onto the fish. Do not refrigerate. Leave the salmon at room temperature until the next morning.
5. The next day, brush the salt off the fish. Wash the fish under cold water and pat dry.
6. Cut off the skin off the fillet. Cut thin slices on an angle and lay them on a serving plate. This is the trickiest and the messiest part of the process so make sure you have a sharp knife.
7. Slice the bagels in half, slather with cream cheese, and top with the lox!

Servings: 4

Choosing the Right Bagel

The one indispensable, perfect breakfast food is the bagel. But which one to choose? The options are limitless, especially if you have a real bagel shop nearby (bagels will keep forever in the fridge). Purists won't touch the blueberry, chocolate chip, whole wheat, sourdough, or even cinnamon raisin for their lox (or other fish) and cream cheese. Others yell, bring on the sweet ones! Whatever you choose, remember that a bagel is like five servings of bread. So choose wisely, and enjoy!

Basic Food Safety Rules

Now that you're finally cooking, there are a few simple rules you must follow. You probably never realized all the careful preparation that went into home-cooked meals, but every Mom (and Dad) knows these safety guidelines. Otherwise, you would have been very sick a long time ago:

- Wash your hands well with warm water and soap before touching anything raw, and when you're done, wash your hands again. Don't bring bacteria into or out of your meals!
- Wipe down your cooking surfaces before and after any food preparation with a nontoxic, soapy solution. This includes your cutting boards, microwave oven, electric grill, and especially your dishes after the meal. Leaving dirty things around is not only disgusting, it's dangerous to your health.
- Make sure eggs and other proteins are fully cooked before you eat them. Invest in a meat thermometer, and use it, whether you are grilling a steak, making chicken, or cooking a ham.

LUNCH

Lunches are a hard meal to manage in college, especially on weekends. If you are sick of dorm food, your meal plan has been cut off, or you can't look at another slice of pizza without instantly gaining five pounds, here are enough recipes for two weeks of tasty and cheap recipes to get you cooking. All of these can be multiplied if you are lucky enough to cook for more than one. These recipes require a weekly grocery trip. Most of these items can be found at a better-than-average convenience store, but you can save money by shopping at a larger establishment. We try to follow the two-bag rule: buy enough food to fill two paper grocery bags. Then you can comfortably carry them home. Or, get a friend to go with you, and

15

you can easily fit four bags in the back of a cab and split the fare. If you have your own car, make a date out of it. Many students are successful meeting up with people by squeezing ripe fruits in the produce aisle. Don't forget to recycle your bags when you're back home.

Creating New Condiments

The "free" food you can remove from your cafeteria can be combined in a host of new ways to spice up any meal. Depending on how much you need, follow the ratios for:

- Russian Dressing: 2 takeout packets mayonnaise to 1 takeout packet ketchup. Add a takeout packet relish if you can find it for the real deal.
- Spicy Asian Glaze: 3 takeout packets soy sauce to 1 takeout packet Chinese or traditional mustard. This works well right before you grill fish, chicken breasts, or pork.
- Special Sauce: 2 takeout packets mayonnaise to 1 takeout packet mustard. Perfect for any sandwich.
- Tuna Helper: 4 takeout packet mayonnaise to 1 takeout packet mustard. Mix with canned tuna to get rid of that "fishy" taste. Add a takeout packet relish if you can find it, if you like your tuna sweet.
- Breakfast Treat: 2 pats butter to 1 takeout packet jelly. Seems obvious, but if you mix these before you spread you will get the perfect combination of sweet and creamy. Or, leave out the jam and add 1 takeout packet honey instead.
- Salsa as Marinade: You'll need at least 5 to 8 takeout packets, but salsa makes a great marinade for fish or chicken.

- Soy as Marinade: You'll need at least 4 takeout packets. Soy sauce is useful in breaking down tougher cuts of beef if used as a marinade. Don't drown the meat in it: simply make sure you have enough to cover both sides, and then rinse off your meat before cooking.
- Salt and Pepper Mix: 2 takeout packets salt to 1 takeout packet pepper. If you can combine these in a single shaker and keep on hand, you can consider yourself an official cook. The recipes in this book mostly omit salt and pepper, so you can add this mix to your taste once your food is cooked.

Green Gazpacho Soup

Green or red, gazpacho soup is a Spanish favorite always eaten cold. It tastes best when it's really cold, so it's a good idea to make it in the morning, right before you leave for your first class. This delicious version can be stored in the refrigerator for up to two days.

Equipment Needed: blender, knife, spoon

Preparation Time: 5 minutes, plus 30 minutes chilling

Ingredients:

1 ripe avocado
1 large cucumber
1 tablespoon white vinegar (white balsamic or apple cider vinegar works as well as the regular distilled variety)
1 takeout packet soup crackers or saltines
Salt and pepper

Preparation:

1. Cut the avocado in half and remove the pit. Scoop out the avocado meat into a blender. Throw away the peel.

2. Peel cucumber and slice in half lengthwise. Run a spoon down the center to remove seeds, which you can discard. Then, cut each half into 1-inch chunks and add to blender.

3. Blend until smooth. If you find that the mixture is too thick (which can happen if the avocado was too large or the cucumber was too small), add a tablespoon of water and blend again for a few seconds. Repeat if necessary.

4. Add vinegar into the blender and blend for 1 minute. Season with salt and pepper.

Food Scraps as Dorm Improvement

An avocado seed can quickly grow into a large, decorative plant. With little care, you can improve your home environment and recycle at the same time. All you need is an empty glass and two forks (borrow all of these items from the cafeteria, you can return them in a few weeks). To start, hold the seed in your hand with the pointed end up, and gently yet forcefully stick each fork into the pit so that it will balance on top of the cup. Fill the cup with water to the point where the bottom third of the seed is covered. Wait until roots grow; this could take a few weeks. You may even see the plant begin to grow from the top first, but wait until the roots are about 3 inches long. Gently remove the forks, and plant in an old coffee can two-thirds filled with soil (you can get both the can and the soil for free, if you're resourceful). Make a small hole in the bottom of the can for drainage and place the can on a shallow plate. Water immediately, and then check the plant to see if it needs more water when the soil looks dry. Find a sunny location in your room and position the plant for maximum sun exposure.

5. Chill the soup for at least 30 minutes in the refrigerator. Pour soup into serving bowls and present with crackers.

Servings: 2

Go-Crazy Swap: For more flavor:

If you have it on hand, throw a garlic clove into the blender at step 4 and blend again for 1 minute. Or, skip the garlic and the salt and pepper, and instead add a pinch of cayenne pepper for a real kick.

Versatile Red Bean Salad

This nutritious, high-protein salad will keep well in the fridge for a day or two.

Equipment Needed: can opener, bowl, fork or spoon, knife, cutting board

Preparation Time: 3 minutes

Ingredients:

> 1 (8-ounce) can red beans, rinsed and drained
> 2 tablespoons white vinegar, any variety
> ½ white onion, chopped
> Large handful walnuts, chopped
> Salt and pepper

Preparation:

1. Smash the red beans in a bowl with a fork or spoon for a few minutes until most of the beans are broken.
2. Add the vinegar.
3. Mix in the onions, walnuts, salt, and pepper.

Servings: 2

Go-Crazy Swap:

This bean salad will also make an excellent spread or dip if you throw all of the ingredients into a blender and mix until you reach a thick yet smooth consistency.

Polish Sausage Hot Dogs

Invite a friend over to study and serve this dish, or halve it if you're eating alone. The remaining sausage can be stored for no more than a week in the refrigerator. If you have a little bit left, you can use as a filling for the next morning's omelet. If you have a lot left, consider inviting your friends over, ordering a large plain pizza, and using the grilled sausage as a fresh topping.

Equipment Needed: electric grill, microwave oven, two microwavable dishes, knife

Preparation Time: 12 minutes

Ingredients:

> 1 precooked turkey Polish sausage
> 3 hot-dog buns
> 1 cup drained sauerkraut
> 3 takeout packets mustard
> 1 cup microwavable chili (one 8-ounce can, or 1 cup from a larger container)

Preparation:

1. Preheat the grill as directed.
2. Cut the sausage into three pieces: each should be about as long as a hot dog. Run a knife through each third lengthwise, splitting the two sides apart gently without separating them.

3. Review the instructions that came with your particular grill. Put the sausage on the grill, sliced side down, and grill for the recommended minutes. Remove from grill.
4. Separate buns for grilling, and place on the grill for 1 minute.
5. Place the sauerkraut in a microwavable dish and microwave on HIGH for 20 seconds. Remove from microwave oven.
6. Pour the chili into a second microwavable dish and warm per instructions on the can.
7. Assemble by putting each sausage into a bun and topping it with one-third of the sauerkraut and one mustard portion. Serve the chili as a side dish.

Servings: 2 to 3

Go-Crazy Swap:

For a different taste, try switching the chili and sauerkraut. Put the chili on the dog, and serve the sauerkraut as a hot or cold side dish.

PhD Hot Soups

What's college life without packaged, dry soups? These staples keep forever, take up little space, and are incredibly handy when you are starving or cold when you come in for lunch. Shop wisely and stock up on your favorites when they are on sale, whether they be ramen noodles, soups in cups or bowls, or packaged classics. Let's take your basic chicken noodle variety and turn it into a heartier meal. The following matrix offers almost instant results.

Equipment Needed: depending on the soup's instructions, either a hot pot or a microwave oven, spoon, knife, cutting board, and an electric grill

Preparation Time: will vary depending on type of soup. Go with instructions on package and add 3 more minutes for preparing additional ingredients

NAME SOUP	INGREDIENTS	PREPARATION	WHAT TO DO WITH LEFTOVERS
Shrimp Soup	1 (1-serving) package chicken noodle soup 6 precooked cocktail shrimp 1 teaspoon dried cilantro	1. Follow the soup package instructions. 2. Once the soup is ready, toss the shrimp into the hot soup and mix carefully with a spoon. 3. Sprinkle cilantro over the soup.	Shrimp spoil quickly: make sure you eat them before their expiration date. Use any remaining shrimp for lunch the next day by mixing with two or three takeout packets mayonnaise and a pinch of cilantro, creating shrimp salad.
Noodle Soup with Sausage	1 (1-serving) package chicken noodle soup 6 ounces grilled Polish sausage (see Polish Sausage Hot Dogs)	1. Follow the soup package instructions. 2. Chop the grilled sausage into ½-inch cubes. 3. Once soup is ready, sprinkle the sausage cubes over the soup and mix carefully. 4. Let stand for 2 minutes so that the flavors mix.	Who ever has leftover sausage? That's like eating half a candy bar.
Chicken Soup with Fresh Veggies	1 (1-serving) package chicken noodle soup ¼ red bell pepper, sliced ¼ cup well-washed fresh spinach, or ⅓ block frozen 3 mushrooms, sliced	1. Follow the soup package instructions. 2. Once soup is ready, sprinkle the vegetables into the soup. Add the spinach separately. Mix carefully until the spinach is wilted or thawed. 3. Let stand for 1 to 3 minutes so that the flavors mix.	Any remaining vegetables can be used as filling for tomorrow's breakfast omelet.

Grilled Portobello Mushroom and Cheese Platter

Grilled vegetables offer a healthy lunch alternative. Buy a few varieties that you can mix and match. However, don't expect veggies to stay fresh for more than a week, even in the refrigerator.

Equipment Needed: electric grill

Preparation Time: 10 minutes

Ingredients:

> 2 tablespoons olive or other vegetable oil
> 1 takeout packet ketchup (or barbecue sauce, if available)
> 1 large portobello mushroom cap
> 2 tablespoons white vinegar (white balsamic or apple cider
> vinegar works as well as the regular distilled variety)
> 2 slices any cheese

Preparation:

1. Preheat the grill as directed.
2. Mix the oil with the ketchup. Coat both sides of the mushroom cap with this mixture.
3. Put the mushroom cap rounded top down on the grill, and grill for 3 to 5 minutes, depending on your grill.
4. Open grill. Carefully pour the vinegar inside the hollow of the cap. Make sure that the liquid stays in the cap. Grill for another minute.
5. Open the grill again, this time placing cheese on the cap, and grill with the top of the grill lowered but not touching the mushroom for 1 minute more, until the cheese just begins to melt.

Servings: 1

> ### Veggie Swap
>
> Portobello mushrooms are very filling, but this recipe would work just as well with any single hearty vegetable. Swap out the mushroom for 1 sliced zucchini, 1 small sliced eggplant, a large handful of fresh spinach, or any amount of leftover vegetables that you might have from another meal. The only thing that's won't work is grilled lettuce!

Fancy Melted Sandwiches

Equipment Needed: electric grill, fork, bowl, can opener

Preparation Time: 5 minutes

Ingredients:

> 1 (1-serving) can or package tuna
> 1 to 2 takeout packets mayonnaise
> 1 takeout packet mustard
> 2 slices any bread
> 2 thin slices any cheese

Preparation:

1. Preheat the grill as directed.
2. Mix together the tuna and one packet mayonnaise with a fork. If it looks too dry for your taste, mix in the second packet of mayonnaise. Then, mix in the mustard.
3. Transfer the tuna mixture onto one slice of bread. Put the cheese slices on top of the tuna.
4. Cover the tuna with the second slice of bread and place on grill. Review grilling instructions. Grill until the bread is crispy and the tuna is warm (usually 3 to 5 minutes).

Servings: 1

Go-Crazy Swap:

Replace tuna with one serving of canned chicken, ham, shrimp, or salmon: they all work great with melted cheese. Or, disregard canned protein altogether and have a plain Jane grilled cheese sandwich!

Chicken Salad Veronique

This salad has a refreshing, sweet taste and can be a very filling meal without bread.

Equipment Needed: knife, bowl, can opener, and cutting board

Preparation Time: 3 minutes

Ingredients:

>1 individual serving-size can diced chicken
>2 takeout packets mayonnaise
>Handful of walnuts, chopped
>½ apple, unpeeled and chopped
>Handful of raisins

Preparation:

1. Place the chicken in a bowl.
2. Mix in the mayonnaise, walnuts, apple, and raisins. Transfer to a plate and serve.

Servings: 1

Super Veggie Burger Wrap

If you are low-carbing, skip the tortilla entirely, but you might want to make two veggie burgers for a lunch that will keep you full until dinner.

Equipment Needed: electric grill, knife, plate

Preparation Time: will depend on package instructions (cooking time depends on the thickness of the patty). Add 5 more minutes to heat the grill and prepare other ingredients.

Ingredients:

> 1 frozen veggie burger patty, or 2 if omitting tortilla
> 1 tortilla wrap
> 1 thin slice any cheese (per patty)
> 2 leaves lettuce
> 2 takeout packets ketchup or barbecue sauce

Preparation:

1. Preheat the grill as directed.
2. Grill veggie burger according to the package instructions (the cooking time depends on the thickness of the patty), cut in half, and transfer to a plate.
3. Grill tortilla separately for 1 minute until warm.
4. Assemble wrap: place the veggie burger in the center of the tortilla, top with cheese, lettuce, and ketchup, and fold over.

Servings: 1

Go-Crazy Swap:

Whatever condiments you've collected can certainly spice up this meal. Don't be afraid to go ethnic. Veggie burger wraps can pass for almost any type of cuisine with a bit of imagination. For a Mexican meal, swap out the ketchup and replace with salsa. For Indian fare, top with chutney instead of ketchup and cheese. For a Chinese flavor, top with hot mustard or sweet-and-sour sauce.

Tips for Tortillas

Packaged tortillas are now a staple at most grocery stores, and you find them in the refrigerated section. If you keep them cool, in the original packaging, and remember to tightly close the package after you remove a tortilla, these babies will last a long time. However, if you've dried yours out accidentally, you can revive them in the microwave oven. Just place a dried tortilla on a microwavable plate, and sprinkle with a little water. Microwave on MEDIUM for about 10 seconds, and you'll see and feel your tortilla come back to life. (This trick works for most kinds of breads, including stale bagels.)

Salad Matrix

If you can get to even the lamest grocery store once a week, you can have a fresh salad meal every day.

Equipment Needed: Knife

Preparation Time: 7 minutes

Preparation:

Follow this matrix to mix and match a variety of salads. Follow the guidelines for the four basic salads and then feel free to embellish with the Go-Crazy list.

NAME	INGREDIENTS	PREPARATION	GO-CRAZY ADD-ONS: ADD ANY COMBINATION OF THESE ITEMS TO ANY OF THE SALADS
Basic Green Salad	½ (10-ounce) package prewashed salad greens 2 tablespoons of your favorite bottled salad dressing	1. Place the salad greens on a plate. 2. Top with any three items from Go-Crazy list. 3. Pour on dressing and serve.	1. ¼ red pepper, diced 2. ½ ripe tomato, sliced 3. ¼ small cucumber, sliced 4. Handful of grated or crumbled cheese 5. Chinese noodles (usually free with a takeout order)
Basic Bean Salad	½ (10-ounce) package prewashed salad greens ½ (8-ounce) can garbanzo or kidney beans, drained and rinsed 1 teaspoon white vinegar (white balsamic or apple cider vinegar works as well as the regular distilled variety)	1. Place the salad greens on a plate. 2. Place rinsed beans on top of the greens. 3. Add any two additional items from Go-Crazy list. 4. Add vinegar, toss salad, and serve.	
Spicy Cabbage Salad	½ (16-ounce) package shredded coleslaw-cabbage mix ¼ onion, finely sliced 1 tablespoon dried oregano 2 tablespoons white vinegar (white balsamic or apple cider vinegar works as well as the regular distilled variety) 1 pinch of red pepper flakes or a few drops of hot sauce (for the brave-hearted)	1. Combine the coleslaw-cabbage mix and onions and put onto a plate. 2. Stir together the oregano, vinegar, and red pepper flakes, and pour over salad.	

NAME	INGREDIENTS	PREPARATION	GO-CRAZY ADD-ONS: ADD ANY COMBINATION OF THESE ITEMS TO ANY OF THE SALADS
Asian Tofu Salad	½ (16-ounce) package of shredded coleslaw cabbage mix ¼ onion, finely sliced ½ (14-ounce) package firm tofu, cut into ½-inch cubes 2 tablespoons soy sauce, or 2 takeout packets	1. Combine the coleslaw cabbage mix and onions, and put on a plate. 2. Place the cubed tofu on top of the coleslaw mixture. 3. Add one item, except for the cheese, from Go-Crazy Add-ons list. 4. Drizzle soy sauce over the salad and serve.	

Peanut Butter 'n' Stuff Sandwiches

Just because you're in college doesn't mean that you can't eat peanut butter sandwiches. You know you still like them! But now that you're on your own, you can use peanut butter as a base to create a more sophisticated lunch.

Equipment Needed: knife, electric grill (optional)

Preparation Time: 2 minutes plain, 6 grilled

Ingredients:

>   2 slices any bread
>   2 tablespoons peanut butter
>   1 tablespoon your favorite jam, or 1 takeout packet

Preparation:
1. Assemble sandwich, just as Mom did.
2. Try toasting your bread first on the electric grill, or make the sandwich and grill it for 1 minute if you like it gooey.

Go-Crazy Swap:

Skip the jam and add up to three items from the following list to jazz up this old standard:

- ½ banana, sliced
- ½ apple, sliced
- 1 tablespoon honey (1.5 takeout packets)
- 1 small handful raisins
- 1 tablespoon chocolate spread or chocolate chips

Dinner

Don't be afraid to make yourself a real dinner. First, it's not any more complicated than lunch. Second, it doesn't have to be any bigger than lunch. And if you still can't get past it, think of making dinner as making a second lunch, just later in the day. The following recipes are so easy; you'll impress yourself, and your friends, in no time at all.

Improving Chili from a Can

Despite its name, you can give this dish a home, and a homemade, taste by adding more vegetables.

Equipment Needed: microwave oven, spoon, can opener, microwavable bowl, or hot pot

31

Preparation Time: Depending on label, but no more than 10 minutes

Ingredients:

> 1 cup microwavable chili, with or without meat.
> ½ green bell pepper, diced
> 2 tablespoons any cheese, shredded*

*The less the manufacturer spends preparing the packaging, the cheaper the cheese will be. Don't be afraid to buy a chunk of cheese and cut the necessary amount off and then dice into little pieces.

Preparation:

1. Transfer the chili into a microwavable dish or directly into the hot pot. Heat the chili according to instructions on the can.
2. When warmed, mix in the green peppers and sprinkle the chili with cheese.

Servings: 1

Go-Crazy Swaps:

Feel free to experiment by adding your favorite veggies, or whatever you have in your mini fridge. Try small thin slices of fresh or canned zucchini, diced mushrooms, diced tomatoes, diced onions, corn, or even diced carrots.

Football Game Hamburgers

Equipment Needed: electric grill, microwave oven, microwavable plates, paper towels, spatula

Preparation Time: 10 minutes

Ingredients:

> 1 pound lean ground beef
> 4 slices bacon
> 4 slices any cheese
> 4 hamburger buns
> 4 leaves lettuce

Preparation:

1. Preheat the electric grill as directed.
2. Separate the ground beef into four portions, and form patties with your hands. Make sure they are the same size as your buns. Do not overhandle or compress the meat too much. If this grosses you out, next time spring for the pre-formed patties.
3. Place all four patties on the grill at the same time. Cook for 5 to 6 minutes depending on the thickness of the burgers. Transfer to a plate.
4. While the burgers are cooking, cook the bacon in the microwave oven. Place bacon on a microwavable plate that is lined with two sheets of paper towel. Microwave on HIGH for 3 minutes. If the bacon is not crispy, cook for an additional 30 seconds. Repeat in 30-second increments until crispy.
5. When the burgers are done, remove, and warm the buns on the grill for 1 to 2 minutes. If you want to melt the cheese on the burger, leave the burgers on the grill and top with cheese. Close the lid of the grill without pressing it for about 1 minute, or until cheese melts. Then, remove burger from grill.
6. Put the burger on the lower part of the bun, topped first by the cheese, then the bacon, and finally a lettuce leaf. Top with the remaining bun.

Servings: 4

Did Someone Say Macaroni and Cheese?

Mac and cheese is the all-time favorite college food. Whatever shape you like, whatever brand you like, you can't beat it for providing a warm and satisfying meal. But did you know that it could actually be improved on? Raid your fridge and pantry, and if you have any of the following items, throw them in!

You can make a whole box of mac and cheese in the hot pot by following the directions on the box. Or, use the single-serving microwavable packages that are now available in stores. If you use the large box, it should make two servings, although we've eaten many a box of mac and cheese by ourselves. Just don't read the calorie information after you've polished off the entire box!

Equipment Needed: microwave oven or hot pot, microwavable bowl, knife, paper towels

Preparation Time: 15 minutes for a large box, shorter if using single-serving microwavable packets

NAME	INGREDIENTS (FOR 1 SERVING)	PREPARATION
Mac and Cheese with Hot Dogs and Peas	1 hot dog, or ¼ Polish sausage if you're really fancy 1 package mac and cheese 1 tablespoon butter pats ¼ cup milk ¼ cup canned peas	1. Cut the hot dog into bite-size pieces 2. Microwave hot dog slices on a paper towel for 45 seconds 3. Prepare mac and cheese according to instructions, adding butter and milk as directed. 4. When fully cooked, mix in peas and hot dog pieces.
Spicy Tuna Noodle Casserole	1 package mac and cheese 1 tablespoon butter, or 2 pats ¼ cup milk 1 (3-ounce) serving tuna fish, drained 2 pieces pickled jalapeño peppers, or 1 packet relish	1. Prepare mac and cheese according to instructions, adding butter and milk as directed. 2. When fully cooked, mix in tuna and jalapeños. 3. Microwave mixture for 1 minute at the power level called for on the package.

NAME	INGREDIENTS (FOR 1 SERVING)	PREPARATION
Tangy Mac and Cheese	1 package mac and cheese ¼ cup sour cream	1. Prepare mac and cheese according to instructions 2. Instead of adding the milk and butter, add the sour cream.

Microwave Madness

The trickiest thing about cooking with your microwave oven is knowing how powerful it is. Not all microwave ovens are created equal, and each will heat up at slightly different time schedules. Undercooking is fine: you can always zap your food again. But once you've overcooked, what was once food is now mush.

It will take about a week to get to know your microwave oven. Experiment, but err on the side of microwaving less. You can always stop the microwave process and test the dish to adjust the cooking or heating time. Good tests are trying to boil a cup of water, or reheating leftovers.

Also important: Do not use any metal wrap or containers with your microwave oven. Always let your food sit for at least one full minute before you try to eat anything that comes out of a microwave oven. And wipe down the inside with a wet paper towel after each use, even if it doesn't "look" dirty.

Mediterranean Pork and Couscous

If you have ever trekked through a desert with a band of Bedouins, you would have had the pleasure of sitting around an open fire and feasting on fantastic grains and grilled goat meat. We're sure that you will find neither a goat nor an open fire on your campus (if you do, call security!). This recipe is as close as we could get to a very exotic dinner in the confines of a dorm.

Equipment Needed: electric grill, hot pot, fork, knife, cutting board

Preparation Time: 20 minutes, but worth the wait

Ingredients:

>   2 cups water
>   1 cup couscous
>   ¼ cup dried cranberries
>   ¼ cup chopped walnuts
>   salt and pepper to taste.
>   4 (6-ounce) pork cutlets, each about ½ inch thick*

* If the cutlets are heavier and/or thicker, you will have to increase the grilling time.

Preparation:

1. Boil the water for the couscous in microwave oven or hot pot.
2. Put the couscous into a heat-proof container that has a lid. Add the cranberries, chopped walnuts, salt, and pepper to the dry couscous. Add the hot water according to the recipe on the box. Cover the container, and let sit for 5 minutes. Fluff out the couscous with a fork when done.
3. Meanwhile, heat the electric grill as directed.
4. Salt and pepper both sides of each pork cutlet.
5. Transfer the cutlets onto the grill and grill for 5 to 7 minutes, until fully cooked. It is very important to fully cook pork.

When you think it is done, pierce with a knife. If juices run clear, you are done. If they are red, cook another 2 minutes and check again. Repeat if necessary.

6. Transfer the cutlets onto clean plates, and serve with couscous as a side dish.

Servings: 4

Hot Tuna and Cold Thai Noodle Salad

Equipment Needed: electric grill, bowl, hot pot, small bowl

Preparation Time: 10–20 minutes, depending on how long it takes to soak the rice noodles

Ingredients:

1 (2-serving) package transparent rice noodles* plus water per package directions
2 tablespoons peanut butter
2 tablespoons water
¼ cup thinly sliced scallions, green parts only
4 tablespoons soy sauce, or 4 takeout packets
1 pound tuna steak**

* You will find these in the Asian section of your grocery store.
** Always make sure you buy fresh fish that does not have a fishy smell. Ask the store clerk to give you a sealed package of ice with your fish. When you get back to your room, keep the tuna on top of that ice in your refrigerator until you are ready to cook. It should be cooked the day it is purchased.

Preparation:

1. Soak the noodles according the package instructions. Read carefully: some require soaking in hot water, while others require cold water. After the noodles are properly soaked, drain and put into a bowl.

2. Meanwhile, mix the peanut butter with the 2 tablespoons water. The peanut butter should now have a consistency similar to a thick pasta sauce; if not, add more water, 1 table-spoon at a time. Add this peanut sauce and the scallions to the noodle bowl. Mix thoroughly, and place in refrigerator until you are ready to serve.
3. Heat electric grill as directed.
4. Drizzle 1 tablespoon of soy sauce onto each side of the tuna steak; place it on the grill. Grill the tuna for 5 to 7 minutes.
5. Remove the grilled tuna and place on a plate. Let it stand for 5 to 10 minutes.
6. Cut the tuna into two pieces and transfer them to separate plates.
7. Divide the cold noodle salad between the two plates. Drizzle remaining soy sauce onto the steaks and the noodle salad.

Servings: 2

Best Chicken Breast Recipes

Once you figure out how to prepare a basic chicken breast and combine it with whatever you have in your refrigerator, you may be known on campus as "the Chef." Be prepared to take on this awesome responsibility.

Equipment Needed: electric grill, two plates

Preparation Time: 10 minutes

Ingredients:

   1 (6-ounce) skinless chicken breast
   1 tablespoon any type of cooking vinegar
   Salt and pepper

Preparation:

1. Preheat the electric grill as directed.
2. Place chicken breast on a plate and sprinkle both sides of the breast with the vinegar.
3. Sprinkle salt and pepper on both sides of the breast.
4. Grill the chicken breast for 4 minutes.
5. Remove to a second, clean plate and let stand for 5 minutes.

Servings: 1

Recipes That Require a Basic Chicken Breast

Use the following matrix to transform your basic chicken breast into something else entirely. Our influences are Italian and Mexican, but you'll quickly get the idea. Basically, think of the lowly chicken breast as a foundation from which great meals can be built. It's also a handy vehicle for your favorite bottled dressing, sauce, or condiment.

Equipment Needed: electric grill, bowls, microwave oven, knife

Preparation Time: no more than 15 minutes each

NAME	INGREDIENTS (FOR 1 SERVING)	PREPARATION
Caesar Chicken Salad	1 recipe Basic Chicken Breast 1 handful prepackaged lettuce ½ small cucumber 3 tablespoons Caesar salad dressing ¼ cup croutons	1. Prepare the chicken breast according to the Basic Chicken Breast recipe. When done, cut the chicken into bite-size pieces. 2. Place the lettuce in a bowl. Peel and slice the cucumber, tossing with the lettuce. Add the chicken. 3. Pour the salad dressing on top, mixing so that the dressing is lightly coating the contents. Top with croutons and serve

NAME	INGREDIENTS (FOR 1 SERVING)	PREPARATION
Chicken Parmesan Sandwich	1 recipe Basic Chicken Breast 3 tablespoons pasta sauce 2 tablespoons shredded mozzarella cheese 1 dinner roll	1. Prepare the chicken breast according to the Basic Chicken Breast recipe. 2. Keep the chicken breast on the electric grill and carefully spread the spaghetti sauce over the breast. Sprinkle it with mozzarella cheese. 3. Lower the lid of the electric grill without touching the top of the chicken breast. Grill for 2 minutes. Remove the chicken breast from grill. 4. Cut the roll in half and warm it on the grill for 1 minute. 5. Transfer the roll to a clean plate. Carefully transfer the chicken breast into the roll and serve.
Chicken Quesadilla	1 recipe Basic Chicken Breast 2 tortillas 2 tablespoons any shredded cheese (Monterey Jack or Cheddar is preferable) ½ teaspoon dried cilantro 2 tablespoons salsa	1. Prepare the chicken breast according to the Basic Chicken Breast recipe. Cut the chicken breast into ½-inch strips. 2. Place one tortilla on the grill. Cover with the chicken strips, and sprinkle the cheese on top. Sprinkle the cheese with the dried cilantro, and cover with the second tortilla. Grill for 2 minutes. 3. Transfer the grilled quesadilla to a large plate and let stand for 2 to 3 minutes. Cut into quarters and serve with salsa on the side for dipping
Chicken Holy Mole—Chicken for Chocolate Lovers	1 recipe Basic Chicken Breast 2 tablespoons chocolate syrup 1 (1-serving) package microwavable white rice water for rice preparation	1. Prepare the chicken breast according to the Basic Chicken Breast Recipe. 2. Before removing the chicken, pour the chocolate syrup on top of chicken. Without closing the top of the grill, heat the chicken breast for another 2 minutes. Remove the chicken from the grill and let stand for 5 to 10 minutes. 3. Prepare the rice according to the package instructions. 4. Serve the chicken with the rice.

Cheap, Fast & Easy Steak Dinner

Steak is one of the easiest meats to cook, particularly on a grill. Although you will not get the charcoal taste you would with an outdoor grill, it will be significantly better than anything from the cafeteria, and maybe even better than what your local restaurant hangout serves.

Equipment Needed: electric grill, knife

Preparation Time: depending on how you like your steak, between 15 and 20 minutes

Ingredients:

> 1 (12-ounce) flank steak, cut in half to fit on the grill
> 2 tablespoons olive oil
> Salt and Pepper to taste
> 2 to 4 teaspoons or takeout packets of your favorite condiment: steak sauce, mustard, or ketchup (optional)

Preparation:

1. Preheat electric grill as directed.
2. Rub the steak on both sides with olive oil. Sprinkle salt and pepper on top of each piece.
3. Grill the steak for 4 to 5 minutes. Open the grill, and poke the steak with a finger to see how resistant it is to the touch. If you like your steak rare, you will want to be able to rest your finger on the meat without resistance. If you like your steak well done, it should feel the firmer to the touch.
4. Serve with your favorite condiment, or just by itself. Good steak doesn't need anything else.

Servings: 2

> ### What Goes with Steak?
>
> Anything you have in your fridge! Use the salad recipes in the lunch chapter and halve them as a perfect side dish. Heat up a can of veggies, such as mushroom slices, carrots, or peas, from your overstocked pantry. If you're really hungry, combine with a half portion of mac and cheese. Sliced raw vegetables with a little salad dressing also make a perfect accompaniment, or try microwavable rice.

Hearty Bulgur Tofu Salad

Equipment Needed: microwave oven, microwavable mixing bowl, spoon

Preparation Time: 20 minutes

Ingredients:

> 2 cups vegetable broth
> 1 cup instant bulgur
> 1 cup firm smoked tofu, cut in ½-inch cubes
> ¼ cup chopped walnuts
> 2 tablespoons of your favorite oil-and-vinegar salad dressing

Preparation:

1. Boil the vegetable broth in a microwavable bowl on HIGH for two minutes. Put bulgur wheat into the bowl and cover with vegetable broth. Let stand according to instructions on the box (about 10 to 15 minutes).
2. When done, stir in the tofu, nuts, and salad dressing. Serve either hot or cold.

Servings: 4

Broccoli and Cauliflower Melt with Bacon

Equipment Needed: microwave oven, microwavable bowl, microwavable lid or plastic wrap, knife, cutting board

Preparation Time: 10 minutes

Ingredients:

> 3 tablespoons any white vinegar
> ½ cup water
> 1 cup broccoli florets (fresh or frozen)
> 1 cup cauliflower florets (fresh or frozen)
> 4 ounces Cheddar cheese
> 1 tablespoon bacon bits

Preparation:

1. Place the water and vinegar into a microwave-safe dish, add broccoli and cauliflower, and toss to coat the vegetables with the liquid.
2. Cover the dish with a microwavable lid or plastic wrap. Microwave the dish on HIGH for 4 to 7 minutes. The broccoli should be bright green and still a bit crispy.
3. Remove and sprinkle the dish with cheese and bacon bits. Serve immediately.

Servings: 2

Go-Crazy Vegetarian:

Not down with dining on imitation swine? Instead of adding bacon bits, bring on half a stick of butter and either a half roll of crushed Ritz crackers or six to eight takeout packets of crackers. Mix these in a small microwavable bowl and microwave for about 30 seconds after the broccoli is cooked (step 2), then pour over the top of the main dish and microwave, along with the cheese, for an additional 60 seconds.

Storing Cheese for the Rest of the Term

Cheese is one of those foods that you would think lasts forever, but it doesn't. Often, even unopened cheese will start to form mold in your refrigerator. To make the most out of your investment, limit the exposure to air and moisture. Soft cheeses like Brie or Muenster will go bad before harder cheeses like Swiss or Cheddar. Soft cheeses need to be wrapped tightly in plastic wrap to keep water and air out, but hard cheeses should be wrapped in parchment paper instead. If you see that your cheese is beginning to grow mold, throw it away.

Baked Sweet Chicken Salad

Equipment Needed: microwave oven, paper towel, microwavable plate, bowl, knife, can opener

Preparation Time: 25 minutes

Ingredients:

> 1 banana, skin still green, ends cut off
> 1 cup water
> 2 teaspoons salt, or 2 takeout packets
> 1 teaspoon butter (½ pat)
> 1 (1-serving) can chicken chunks
> 1 teaspoon any dried herbs (parsley, cilantro, dill)

Preparation:

1. Place the banana, unpeeled, on a microwave-safe dish, cutting off the tips. Cover with a paper towel and microwave on HIGH for 3 minutes, or until the skin opens up.
2. Let cool, peel off the skin, and add the water to the same dish. Microwave on HIGH for 4 minutes.
3. Transfer the banana to a clean mixing bowl, reserving the liquid.
4. Add the salt and mash with a fork.
5. Add the butter, chicken, and herbs. Mix all the ingredients until they stick together.

Servings: 1

The Pasta Matrix

Any type of pasta can be made in the microwave oven. However, small or thin pastas, like orzo or thin spaghetti, will become very soft and mushy. We suggest using a larger variety, like penne, ziti, or thick spaghetti. You can also use noodles from your favorite ramen noodle package. Just put the flavoring packet aside and prepare the noodles according to the package instructions.

Equipment Needed: microwave oven, microwavable bowl

Preparation Time: 7 to 10 minutes

Basic Ingredients:

>   2 cups water
>   8 ounces pasta
>   ½ cup your favorite pasta sauce *or*
>   2 tablespoons butter (3 pats) *or*
>   2 tablespoons olive oil *or*
>   Parmesan cheese, grated (optional)

Preparation:

1. Place the water into a microwave-safe dish. Boil according to microwave instructions, usually on HIGH for 2 minutes.
2. Carefully, place the pasta into the bowl and microwave on HIGH for an additional 5 minutes. Test for doneness and repeat in 2-minute increments if necessary. Drain and serve with your preferred topping.

Servings: 1

Use the following matrix to make a more interesting pasta meal. If you prefer to eat your meal piping hot, put the dish back into the microwave oven and heat on HIGH for 15-second increments until it reaches the desired temperature.

NAME	INGREDIENTS	PREPARATION
Pasta Puttanesca	8 ounces pasta 2 cups water 1 tablespoon capers 1 heaping tablespoon chopped olives Pinch of dried oregano 2 tablespoons olive oil	1. Following basic instructions, cook the pasta, omitting its basic toppings. 2. Mix the capers, olives, and oregano with the oil. 3. Add the drained pasta, toss, and serve.

NAME	INGREDIENTS	PREPARATION
Pasta with Broccoli Pesto	8 ounces pasta 2 cups water to cook pasta, plus ½ cup to cook broccoli ¾ cup broccoli florets 2 teaspoons Parmesan cheese, grated 1 clove garlic, peeled and chopped 1 tablespoon olive oil	1. Following basic instructions, cook the pasta, omitting its basic toppings. 2. Put the broccoli into a second microwavable dish with the ½ cup water and microwave on HIGH for 5 minutes or until done. 3. Allow the broccoli to cool for 5 minutes. 4. Reserving the water from the broccoli, in a blender, mix the broccoli with the Parmesan cheese, garlic, and olive oil. If the sauce does not have a liquid consistency, mix in the reserved broccoli water, 1 teaspoon at a time. 5. Toss over the drained pasta and serve.
Pasta with Feta Cheese and Walnuts	8 ounces pasta 2 cups water 2 tablespoons olive oil 2 tablespoons crumbled feta cheese 1 tablespoon chopped walnuts 1 tablespoon dried herbs (cilantro, mint, or parsley)	1. Following basic instructions, cook the pasta, drain, coat with the oil, and let cool. 2. Add the crumbled feta cheese, chopped walnuts, and herbs; toss and serve.
Pasta with Pinto Beans and Spinach	8 ounces pasta 2 cups water 3 tablespoons canned pinto beans, rinsed and drained 1 handful prewashed spinach 3 tablespoons tomato sauce 2 tablespoons olive oil	1. Following basic instructions, cook the pasta, omitting its basic toppings. 2. Drain pasta and mix in all remaining ingredients. 3. Heat for 20 seconds on HIGH in microwave oven, repeat in 10-second intervalsas necessary, to heat all ingredients through.
Leftovers Pasta Salad	1 serving cold, cooked pasta 1 (1-serving) can salmon or tuna packed in oil, drained ½ cup any leftover vegetables, including olives, diced peppers, diced zucchini, diced carrots Salt and pepper	Combine all ingredients in a bowl and serve.

One-Dish Rice Dinners

All the rice recipes in this section call for brown rice, which is healthier and more filling. The recipes are designed so that the only ingredient that must be cooked is rice. The rest of the ingredients are mixed in after the rice is cooked and heated if necessary.

Equipment Needed: microwave oven, 3-quart microwavable bowl with lid or plastic wrap, fork, knife, cutting board

Preparation Time: Time will depend on the type of rice that is purchased. We recommend the instant variety because it is precooked. However, below you'll also find instructions for cooking brown rice in case you cannot find the instant variety. If you can find the instant variety, follow the instructions on the package.

Ingredients:

> 1 cup uncooked brown rice (yields about 3 to 4 cups cooked rice)
> 2 ¼ cups water or broth
> 1 tablespoon butter (1.5 pats)

Preparation: Combine the rice, liquid, and butter, in a 3-quart microwavable dish and cover. Microwave on HIGH for 4 minutes or until the water is boiling. Switch to MEDIUM and continue to cook for 30 minutes. When done, fluff with a fork.

Servings: 2

NAME	INGREDIENTS	PREPARATION
Rice and	1 cup uncooked rice	1. Prepare the rice with the water and butter as directed.
Beans	2¼ cups water or broth 1 tablespoon butter, or 3 pats	2. Heat the beans in the microwave oven on HIGH for 15-second intervals until hot.

NAME	INGREDIENTS	PREPARATION
	½ cup any beans, rinsed and drained ½ teaspoon cumin Pinch of chili powder Pinch of dried green herbs, such as parsley	3. Mix the hot rice, beans, cumin, chili powder, and green herbs, and serve.
Cold California Rice Salad	1 cup cold, cooked rice ¼ avocado, chopped 1 tablespoon canned corn, drained ½ cup chopped watercress Salt and pepper to taste	Combine all ingredients and serve at room temperature.
Chinese Brown Rice with Shrimp	1 cup cooked rice 4 medium-size cooked shrimp 1 tablespoon soy sauce, or 1 takeout packet ¼ teaspoon minced ginger ½ tablespoon any white vinegar	Mix together all ingredients, and heat in microwave on HIGH for 30-second intervals until warm.
African Brown Rice	1 cup uncooked rice 2¼ cups water or broth 1 tablespoon butter, or 3 pats Pinch of cinnamon 1 tablespoon crushed nuts, any kind 1 tablespoon any dried fruit or berries (apricots, dates, figs, raisins, cranberries) ½ cup chopped, cooked chicken breast	1. Prepare the rice with the water and broth as directed and sprinkle with the cinnamon. 2. Mix in nuts, dried fruit, and chicken. 3. Heat the rice for 15 seconds or until the rice achieves desired temperature.
Asian Rice and Tofu Salad	½ teaspoon sesame oil (use any vegetable oil if not available) ½ tablespoon soy sauce, or ½ takeout packet 1 cup cooked rice ½ cup firm tofu, drained and cut into 1/2-inch cubes	1. Combine liquid ingredients and mix into cooked rice. 2. Add tofu and heat in microwave oven on HIGH for 15 seconds and stir. If the dish is not hot enough, heat again for 10-second intervals until the dish reaches desired temperature.
Rice and Turkey Stew	1 (8-ounce) can tomato soup ½ cup cooked rice ½ cup chopped smoked turkey	1. Combine all ingredients in a microwavable bowl. 2. Heat in microwave on HIGH for 3 minutes. The soup should have a thick, stew-like consistency.

White vs. Brown Rice

The difference between white rice and brown rice is simple: Brown rice is considered a healthy grain, white rice is not. Brown rice has more nutrients than white because it still has the bran layer and the germ of the rice grain attached to it; white rice has these layers removed. White rice has less fiber and fewer vitamins than brown, but is still an excellent source of niacin and a moderate source of protein. When cooking the brown rice, use a 1:2 ratio of rice to liquid. However, when cooking white rice, a 1:1 ratio should be used and the cooking time may need to be reduced by 30 percent.

Snacks and Study Breaks

Other cookbooks would call these side dishes, but we know that these recipes come in handy when you are on the go and may often end up being an entire meal. Use the following recipes however you see fit. Pair with a dinner or lunch to create a bigger meal, or eat alone after classes to tide you over until your next cafeteria meal.

Fruit Salad Snack

Many corner delis and grocery stores now provide fruit salads that are cut and ready to be eaten out of plastic transparent containers. However, there is nothing like homemade fruit salad: it is likely to be fresher, less expensive, and have only the fruit that you like.

Equipment Needed: knife, bowl

Preparation Time: 3 to 5 minutes

Ingredients:

Here are my three favorite combinations:

⅓ cup each, sliced:

- Apple, orange, and banana
- Strawberries, blueberries, and banana
- Cantaloupe, mango, and blueberries
- Grapes, pear, and apple
- Peach, strawberries, and raspberries

Preparation: Wash the fruit before cutting. Do not wash more then you will be using. Make sure that the berries do not stand in water because excessive water exposure can make them soggy. Cut all fruits, combine, and eat. Do not make more than you will eat: fruit salad will not last longer than 2 days.

Servings: 1

How to Eat or Serve a Mango: Katie D. Reflects

I never saw a mango before I was twenty-one. I had just graduated from college, and I was on a crazy all-fruit diet. I was attracted to the mango because of its large size. Unfortunately, I didn't have a clue how to eat it. So I sat at my desk and took a bite, like I was eating a peach. Big mistake: the skin was like leather, the juice ran all over my outfit, and the mango shredded into a stringy mess that got stuck in between my teeth. Needless to say, that was the end of my all-fruit diet, and more, I didn't try a mango again for a long time.

Now I know better, and mangoes are my favorite fruit. Just so you don't make the same mistake, you need to know that a mango has (1) a long, thick pit inside that does not like to be separated from the flesh of the fruit; and (2) thick skin that you are not supposed to eat! The easiest way to get to the meat of this fruit is to take a sharp knife and slice through the middle of the fruit along the pit. Start with the side without the pit: peel back the skin with your hand, or with the knife. Then, dice the mango. For the side with the pit, it's best just to cut out the pit and throw it away and repeat the dicing.

Papaya—Brazilian Style

There are snacks and then there are snacks. We tried this one on the streets of São Paulo, Brazil, during the carnival season. If you have a papaya, this is a refreshing and very filling snack.

Equipment Needed: knife, spoon

Preparation Time: 1 minute

Ingredients:

> 1 medium-size papaya*
> ¼ lemon, or 1 tablespoon lemon juice

*Make sure that the papaya is ripe when you buy it. If it is not soft to the touch, leave it outside the refrigerator for a day or two before eating it. Don't worry if it develops a few dots of brown on the skin.

Preparation:

1. Cut the papaya in half. Use a spoon to scoop out the black seeds and the stringy insides. Try not to take out the papaya pulp.
2. Sprinkle the lemon juice over the papaya and eat with a spoon by scooping out the fruit pulp. Try not to scoop out the rind; it can be bitter.

Servings: 2

What to do with leftovers:

Papaya is a wonder fruit, and it may come in large sizes. If you are eating only one serving, you can use the remaining half the following morning as a yogurt topping or in a smoothie. Just keep the leftovers in a refrigerator, and as with the mango, remember to peel off the skin before using.

Popcorn for All Occasions

Microwavable popcorn comes in many different flavors and can be enjoyed on its own. However, if you are adventurous and would like to serve popcorn with a theme, or if you are just bored of the same old, same old, here is a matrix that can be useful.

Equipment Needed: microwave oven, a very large bowl, microwavable cup

Preparation Time: depending on popcorn instructions, but no more than 10 minutes.

OCCASION	INGREDIENT(S) FOR OCCASION
Fall Harvest Party	1 cup nuts ½ cup chocolate chips ½ cup honey
No other dessert around	1 tablespoon confectioners' sugar 1 teaspoon lemon juice 1 teaspoon vanilla extract

OCCASION	INGREDIENT(S) FOR OCCASION
We were going to have Italian food, but we're too cheap	2 tablespoons finely graded Parmesan cheese 1 teaspoon dried parsley or oregano
Hot Valentine Snack	⅓ teaspoon chili powder ½ teaspoon paprika

Ingredients:

2 tablespoons butter (3 pats)
1 bag plain, unsalted microwavable popcorn (which makes approximately 6 cups popcorn)

Preparation:

1. Put the butter in a microwavable cup and melt in the microwave oven on MEDIUM for 1 minute. If the butter is not completely melted, swish it around in the cup. It will melt without more cooking by the time you are ready to use it.
2. Microwave the popcorn per the instructions on the package.
3. Meanwhile, combine melted butter with the Occasion ingredients.
4. When the popcorn has finished cooking, carefully open the package and pour into the large bowl, removing any unpopped kernels. Then, drizzle the butter mixture over the popcorn, carefully tossing to coat.

Servings: 6

Finish-Your-Breakfast Trail Mix

The number one lesson we learned in college was to Plan Ahead. If you are going to be cramming for a test (or writing papers, going to late-night parties...you name the reason and it was one of ours), bring something to eat! That way, you don't have waste time in the cafeteria, or scrounging through your friend's place only to find saltines or American cheese singles. You can take this snack anywhere, and it is a good boost whenever you are missing a meal, whether it's breakfast, lunch, dinner, or beyond.

Equipment Needed: a zip-top plastic bag

Preparation Time: 2 minutes

Ingredients:

> 1 cup O's-type cereal
> 1 cup any other crunchy cereal except flakes
> 1 cup pretzels nuggets, sticks, or bowties
> ½ cup raisins
> ½ cup chocolate chips

Preparation: Mix the ingredients in a large zip-top plastic bag. Stick it in your backpack, and eat as necessary.

Servings: 1 (you don't have to share)

More Nachos Please

Equipment Needed: microwave oven, microwavable dish

Preparation time: 1 to 2 minutes

Ingredients:

> 20 tortilla chips
> 4 ounces any cheese (preferably Cheddar), shredded
> Salsa

Preparation:

1. Place chips on a microwavable dish and liberally sprinkle with cheese.
2. Cook in microwave oven on MEDIUM for 1 minute, or until the cheese has melted. Increase time in 30-second increments if necessary. There's nothing worse than burnt, microwaved cheese.
3. Serve with salsa on the side.

Servings: 1

More Nacho Toppings

When you are making nachos, the tempting smell of warm cheese may make you realize that you are much hungrier than you thought. Instead of whipping up another portion, just add any of the following to the heated nachos to make a meal out of the snack:

- ½ avocado, chopped
- pickled jalapeño peppers, sprinkled to your liking
- 1 can refried beans, heated in microwave in a microwave-safe dish (not in the can)
- diced tomatoes, peppers, or onions

Dried Fruit Mix

Another take-it-with-you snack. Feel free to share this one; at least it's good for you!

Equipment Needed: bowl, zip-top plastic bag

Preparation Time: 2 minutes

Ingredients:

> 1 cup dried apricots
> ½ cup dried cranberries
> ½ cup almonds, whole or slivered
> ½ cup chopped walnuts
> 1 rice cake, plain or cinnamon, honey, or other dessert

Preparation: Mix the ingredients in a large zip-top plastic bag to take with you. Keep any remaining dried fruits in the fridge: they will last forever and not get as sticky over time.

Servings: 1 or more if you share

Peanut Butter Apple Slices

Equipment Needed: sharp knife, spoon

Preparation Time: 2 minutes

Ingredients:

> 1 apple, any variety
> 1 tablespoon peanut butter, smooth or chunky

Preparation:

1. Cut apple into six slices, removing the core and seeds.
2. Spread the peanut butter over the slices, and eat.

Servings: 1

Not-Quite-Texas Toast

This is not exactly a traditional Texas recipe. However, we learned it from a woman who was six months pregnant at the time, and living in Austin. Despite our fears that pregnant women will eat really weird stuff, this snack was amazing!

Equipment Needed: electric grill

Preparation Time: 5 minutes

Ingredients:

> 1 slice whole-grain bread (best if it has nuts and/or visible grains)
> 1 (2-ounce)slice any cheese
> 2 ounces fresh beansprouts

Preparation:

1. Preheat electric grill as directed
2. Place the bread on the grill and grill for 2 minutes.
3. Place the cheese on the toast and lower the top of the grill without touching the cheese and grill until the cheese softens, approximately 1 to 2 minutes.
4. Take toast off the grill, and top with the sprouts.

Servings: 1

What Is Texas Toast?

Traditional Texas toast is simply white bread that has been coated with garlic butter on both sides and grilled. It is usually served with barbecue, but sounds delicious enough to eat on its own. To make the real thing, all you need is your electric grill and the following ingredients:

1. 1 tablespoon butter, or 2½ pats of, at room temperature
2. 1 clove garlic, minced, or 1 teaspoon garlic powder
3. Salt and freshly ground pepper
4. 1 slice white bread

PREPARATION: Preheat your grill as directed. Mix together the butter and garlic, and season with salt and pepper. Coat both sides of the bread with the butter mixture and place on the grill, lowering the lid. Grill the bread for 1 to 2 minutes until lightly golden brown.

Any Veggie with Tofu Dip

Enjoy this dip with whatever you've got in the fridge: Sliced or small carrots, rings of zucchini, celery stacks, cauliflower florets, large slices of peppers, salad greens, or tomatoes.

Equipment Needed: bowl, fork

Preparation Time: 5 to 10 minutes

Ingredients:

1 box silken tofu
3 teaspoons honey mustard
2 tablespoons soy sauce, or 2 takeout packets

2 tablespoons olive oil

1 tablespoon any savory dried herbs (parsley, cilantro, or chives)

Preparation:

1. Drain tofu, place it into a bowl, and crush with a fork.
2. Mix the honey mustard with soy sauce and olive oil. Add to tofu and mix with fork.
3. Add the herbs and mix well. If the mixture is not smooth enough, add 1 teaspoon water and mix again. Repeat as necessary.

Servings: 4

Spicy Pumpkin Seeds

This is the follow-up snack to a really successful Halloween. Even if you don't dress up, making pumpkin seeds is a must-do experience. If you like it, you can continue the fun throughout the fall, as long as pumpkins are available.

Equipment Needed: microwave oven, microwavable bowl

Preparation Time: 15 to 20 minutes

Ingredients:

1 tablespoon ground cinnamon

1 teaspoon ground cumin

¼ cup apple cider vinegar

2 cups fresh pumpkin seeds, dried

Preparation:

1. Combine the cinnamon, cumin, and vinegar in a microwavable bowl.
2. Add pumpkin seeds and mix. Let stand for 10 minutes.

3. Microwave the coated seeds on HIGH for 4 minutes.
4. Stir and microwave at HIGH for an additional 2 minutes. Repeat this step in 2-minute intervals until the seeds are golden brown and crunchy.

Servings: 2

Food Scraps as Dorm Improvement, Take Two— How to Carve a Pumpkin

Unless you were watching your parents carefully over the years, you might not really know how to carve a pumpkin. All you need is a sharp knife, a large bowl, a garbage pail at the ready, a felt-tip pen, and a little imagination. To begin, pick a pumpkin with a flat bottom so it can stand on its own. Then, cut a circle around the stem, large enough to fit your hand through once it's removed. Remove the stem, and set aside. Roll up your sleeves and reach in, grabbing anything you can. You will be taking out the stringy wet mess as well as the seeds. Dump everything into the bowl, and continue until the pumpkin is empty. Scrape off the goop from the top of the pumpkin as well.

When you're done, run a paper towel around the inside of the pumpkin so that you can feel that you've got everything out, and that you are working with a clean interior. Use your felt-tip pen to plan a picture to cut out. Cut along the lines, to get the desired effect. If you feel really spooky, put a lit candle in a small container inside the pumpkin, and put the top back on. Voilà, you're ready for Halloween.

Back to the seeds: Separate the goop from the seeds with your hands. Throw the goop away in the garbage, and place the seeds in a strainer or on a paper towel. When you've separated them all out, rinse them well and pat dry. You're ready for the Spicy Pumpkin Seeds recipe.

White Fondue

Equipment Needed: microwave oven, microwave-safe dish, knife, fork

Preparation Time: 10 minutes

Ingredients:

> 1 (8-ounce) sweetened condensed milk
> 5 drops vanilla extract
> 1 firm pear, peeled, cored, and cut into thick strips
> 1 cup strawberries, washed and trimmed

Preparation:

1. Transfer the condensed milk into a microwave-safe dish and heat on MEDIUM for 30 seconds. The condensed milk should be warm, not hot. Add the vanilla extract, and stir.
2. Dip the fruit into the mixture with a fork.

Servings: 2

PARTY FOOD

The keys to a great party are lots of music and lots of food, and preferably the two can complement each other. Everybody loves a theme! The following are not mere recipes: think of them as the backbone to guaranteed party success.

It's a good idea to assume that your guests are arriving hungry. Whatever you choose to serve, if the recipe says it will serve the exact number of people you have invited, then double the recipe. Plan ahead: do the math before you go shopping. Remember that any good party will draw lots of uninvited attendees, a.k.a. party crashers. If you're prepared, it won't be a problem.

Ole! Mexican Fiesta Theme

A Mexican theme party can work any time of the year, but will be particularly inspired right after Halloween on November 1–2, which is not only All Saints' Day, but more commonly known South of the Border as the Day of the Dead (Dia de los Muertos). Other popular choices would be May 5 (Cinco de Mayo), or September 16 (Mexican Independence Day).

Fresh Guacamole and Chips

There's nothing worse that buying premade guacamole, only to open the container and find out that it's spoiled. Avoid this party disaster by preparing your own. Make sure you have lots of chips on hand (you were going to buy those anyway).

Equipment Needed: bowl, knife, spoon

Preparation Time: 5 minutes to prepare, 5 minutes to sit

Ingredients:

>   2 ripe avocados
>   1 medium-size red onion, peeled and diced
>   1 medium-size tomato, diced with excess liquid removed
>   1 tablespoon lemon juice
>   2 to 4 drops hot sauce, depending on how brave you are

Preparation:

1.   Slice the avocados in half, removing the pits. Do not throw out the pits; you will put the pits back into the finished guacamole until the party begins. The guacamole is less likely to turn dark if the pits remain in the dish. Don't ask why, but it works.
2.   Mash the avocados in a bowl and then stir in the onion, tomato, and lemon juice. Add the hot sauce one drop at a time and thoroughly mix in. Taste and add more hot sauce

if necessary. You want to achieve a spicy but not overbear-
ing flavor.

3. Add the avocado pits into the bowl and cover the bowl with
   plastic wrap. Stick the bowl in the fridge for at least 5 minutes
   for the flavors to come together, or until the party starts.

Servings: 15

Homemade Salsa

Even if your month-old jar of salsa looks OK; it is probably spoiled,
with a vinegar taste and smell. You can spring for a couple of new
jars, but it's cheaper and tastier to make it yourself.

Equipment Needed: bowl, knife, spoon, cutting board

Preparation Time: 10 minutes

Ingredients:

> 2 tomatoes, diced
> 1 jalapeño pepper, diced (if jalapeños aren't available, sub-
> stitute a green or yellow bell pepper)
> 1 medium-size onion, diced
> 1 teaspoon dried cilantro
> ½ (15-ounce) can corn (drained)

Preparation: Mix all of the ingredients in a bowl. As they settle,
the vegetables will sweat, or produce excess liquid. This is not a
problem.

Servings: 10

Jalapeño Safety

Many people are afraid of jalapeño peppers. In fact, they are not the most spicy variety in the pepper family (Scotch bonnets seem to be the true winner). When jalapeños are properly prepared, they can actually be eaten raw, all by themselves. Start by slicing the jalapeño in half, and carefully remove all the seeds with the tip of your knife. Then, slice across the pepper very finely, no more than ⅛ inch in thickness. Make sure you wash your hands right after handling these peppers, because the oil secreted can cause a burning sensation on the skin or in the eyes.

All-American Party Theme

Think tailgating before the big game, Fourth of July party in the dead of winter, Election Day, Memorial Day, or Veteran's Day. You get the idea.

Mini Cheese Dogs

Because this dish cooks very quickly and should be served hot, prepare the ingredients beforehand, then microwave the dish just as the guests arrive.

Equipment Needed: microwave oven, two microwavable bowls, spoon, toothpicks for serving

Preparation Time: 5 minutes

Ingredients:

1 (12-ounce) package mini hot dogs, each cut in half
1 pound processed cheese, cubed (American cheese or mild
Cheddar are best)
2 tablespoons dried cilantro

Preparation:

1. Microwave the hot dogs on HIGH for 1 minute. Set aside in a clean serving bowl.
2. Microwave cheese on HIGH for 2 minutes or until cheese is completely melted. Stir the cheese after the first 2-minute interval, and if necessary continue to heat 1 minute at a time, stirring after each minute. When cheese is completely melted, stir in the cilantro.
3. Insert toothpicks into the hot dogs, place them next to the bowl of melted cheese, and serve.

Servings: 12

Never-Fail Party Planning Advice

Great parties depend on flow. You want people to mingle, dance, and flirt. What you don't want are vultures hovering over your food all night, or bored guests sitting on the couch and not moving. The best way to ensure party flow is to separate the food and beverages in the opposite corners of the party room. That way people will be constantly moving, creating "good party flow." And don't forget plenty of napkins, cups, and ice!

Spicy Grilled Chicken Wings

Equipment Needed: small bowl, zip-top plastic bag, electric grill, paper towels

Preparation Time: 10 minutes to assemble, 1 hour to marinate, less than 10 minutes for each grilled batch

Ingredients:

> 2 tablespoons vegetable oil
> 2 tablespoons Worcestershire sauce
> 1 tablespoon hot sauce
> 4 pounds fresh chicken wings (about 24 pieces)
> 1 cup of bottled blue cheese dressing
> Celery sticks

Preparation:

1. In a small bowl, stir together the oil, Worcestershire sauce, and hot sauce. Taste: if you can handle a spicier sauce, add more hot sauce, but no more than 5 drops at a time. Mix thoroughly, and retest until you are satisfied.
2. Put the chicken wings in the plastic bag and pour in the marinade. Seal and shake the bag to distribute the marinade. Refrigerate the bag for at least 1 hour, shaking it occasionally. Separately refrigerate dressing and celery sticks during the marinating process.
3. Preheat electric grill as directed.
4. Remove the wings from the marinade and pat them dry with paper towels. Throw out remaining marinade: do not use as a basting sauce because it may contain bacteria from the raw chicken.
5. Arrange as many wings as can fit on the grill. Close the grill and cook for 5 minutes. Repeat with the remaining wings.
6. Serve with the blue cheese dressing and celery sticks.

Servings: 6, assuming 3 to 4 pieces per person

Green Dip

This dip is the perfect companion to a vegetable platter and will also go well with potato or corn chips. Any leftovers can be used as a fresh salad dressing. But eat it soon: it can only be kept in the refrigerator for a few days.

Equipment Needed: blender, bowl, knife, cutting board

Preparation Time: 5 to 10 minutes

Ingredients:

> ½ cup fresh cilantro, chopped, stems removed
> ½ cup fresh parsley, chopped, stems removed
> 4 cloves garlic, peeled and sliced
> 1 cup sour cream
> 1 tablespoon grated Parmesan cheese

Preparation:

1. Put all the ingredients in the blender and turn on for 30 seconds, or until the contents are incorporated. The mixture should still be thick, but have taken on a green color from the cilantro and parsley.
2. Transfer the mixture into a bowl and serve.

Servings: 10

Create a Colorful Veggie Platter

The first rule is use whatever you've got. Veggie platters are a great way to get rid of leftovers. If you need to start shopping, choose three varieties from this list. Choose a mix of bold colors for the best presentation, and buy what looks and smells freshest:

- baby carrots
- cucumber or zucchini, cut into disks or squared slices
- celery sticks, cut into 3- to 4-inch lengths
- button mushrooms
- sugar snap peas
- red or yellow bell peppers
- broccoli florets (discard stems)

Formal Entertaining

Every once in a while, it's actually nice to get out of your jeans and sneakers and into more formal attire, even if its only switching to jeans and boots or sandals (weather permitting). For a more sophisticated evening, impress your friends with these recipes, which are just as cheap, fast, & easy as the others.

Mushroom Caps with Goat Cheese

Equipment Needed: microwave oven, paper towel, microwavable plate, teaspoon, bowl

Preparation Time: 4 minutes

Ingredients:

30 white (button) or brown (baby bella) mushrooms

1 pound packaged goat cheese (if not available, substitute a mix of 2 cups ricotta cheese and 1 cup Parmesan cheese)
2 tablespoons dried cilantro

Preparation:

1. Wipe each mushroom cap gently with a moist paper towel. Gently remove the mushroom stems and place the caps, facing upward, onto a microwavable plate. Set aside.
2. In a bowl, mix the goat cheese with the cilantro.
3. Using a teaspoon, fill the mushroom caps with the cheese mixture. Make sure the cheese lands within the confines of the hole created by the missing stem and is not flowing over the sides of the mushroom.
4. Cook in microwave on MEDIUM for 1 minute, or until the cheese begins to melt. If additional time is required, add in increments of 30 seconds.

Servings: 15

Salami and Daikon Rolls

Daikon is a readily available Japanese radish. It is a long, white root vegetable with a crispy texture and a bit of a tangy flavor.

Equipment Needed: knife, vegetable peeler

Preparation Time: less than 10 minutes

Ingredients:

1 large daikon, washed, peeled, and sliced into ¼-inch rounds (if you cannot find daikon, substitute jicama—a Mexican root vegetable that can also be peeled and sliced)
1 foot-long salami or pepperoni, sliced into ¼-inch rounds
2 takeout packets mustard

Preparation:

1. Lay out the daikon slices on the serving plate.
2. Put a drop of mustard on each daikon slice.
3. Cover each with a round of the salami, and serve.

Servings: 10

Sophisticated Cheese Platter

Equipment Needed: three knives, vegetable peeler, serving plate or platter

Preparation Time: 2 minutes

Ingredients:

> 1 pound Brie cheese
> 1 pound sharp Cheddar cheese, left as a block
> 1 pound Swiss cheese, left as a block
> 1 baguette French bread (if you cannot find fresh French bread, substitute 1 box of your favorite hearty crackers)
> 2 large cucumbers, peeled and sliced into ¼-inch rounds

Preparation:

1. Place three cheeses on a plate, each with their own knife. If you are worried about having knives out at a party, you should either reevaluate serving this to your friends, or your friends in general.
2. Put cucumber slices next to the cheese. Carb-conscious guests will use these instead of bread or crackers.
3. Cut the French bread into thin slices, preferably on an angle. Place bread in a bowl next to the cheese plate.

Servings: 15

Endive Cheese and Fruit Boats

When buying the endive, choose a firm one that looks on the larger side. The leaves must be large enough to cradle the other ingredients.

Equipment Needed: knife, paper towels, cutting board, 2 plates

Preparation Time: 15 minutes

Ingredients:

> 1 endive
> 2 tablespoons olive oil
> ¼ pound blue cheese
> 1 firm pear (Bosc is an excellent choice for this recipe), cut in half, cored, and sliced into thin strips
> 6 fresh mint leaves, finely chopped, or 1 tablespoon dried

Preparation:

1. Cut off the stem of the endive and gently separate the leaves. Discard the top leaves, and rinse and dry the rest on paper towels.
2. Arrange the endive leaves face up on a large flat plate or tray. Drizzle a few drops of olive oil inside the endive leaves.
3. Crumble the blue cheese onto a different plate. Transfer 1 teaspoon of cheese into each endive leaf. Top with a pear slice, and sprinkle with the mint.

Servings: 10+

Rice Pudding Sundae

A dessert course can send everyone home feeling satisfied. This recipe is fun for guests to prepare themselves, which cuts down on your prep time. Just make sure you have enough bowls for the ingredients.

Equipment Needed: spoons, three serving bowls

Preparation Time: 2 minutes

Ingredients:

> 1 (22-ounce) tub prepared rice pudding (found in refrigerated section)
> 1 pint strawberries, washed, stems removed, and sliced
> 9 ounces mixed nuts, unsalted (although salted is fine)
> 1 (16-ounce) bottle chocolate syrup
> 1 small tub whipped topping

Preparation:

1. Place the rice pudding, strawberries, and mixed nuts in individual serving bowls.
2. Instruct the guests to put 2 tablespoons of rice pudding into their cups, and top it with the strawberries, mixed nuts, and a drizzle of chocolate syrup. Top with a dollop of whipped cream.

Servings: 12

When the Party's Really Over

Why is it that at every party there's at least one guest who has overstayed his or her welcome? It's hard to be tactful and polite when you want to go to sleep, especially when someone isn't taking your subtle hints. My advice is simple: throw the offending partier his or her coat, and point to the door. If the guest didn't bring a coat, it's a bit harder; but, still muster the courage to show him or her the door. Or, if you really want to get the dawdler to leave in a hurry, ask him or her to help clean up!

DESSERT

Now the fun really begins! Everyone likes to make dessert, and since there is no baking, there's nothing to be afraid of. These recipes are easy enough to make for one, but once you're in the mix, you might as well double or triple the recipe and make these for your friends. See how popular you'll become once everyone knows who's storing the whipped cream!

It's Officially Dessert

Beyond the division of "red" and "blue" states, some states in both camps have taken a strong position on what they consider to be a proper dessert. The following lists several that have amended their constitutions in favor of an official state flavor:

- Massachusetts has a state dessert, Boston cream pie, as well as a state cookie, the chocolate chip cookie (which was invented in 1930 at the Toll House Restaurant in Whitman, Massachusetts).
- Minnesota has designated the blueberry muffin as its official state muffin. However, the legislature did not go as far as to mention when blueberry muffins should be eaten: breakfast, lunch, snack, or dessert.
- New Mexico's state cookie is the biscochito, a traditional cookie flavored with anise and cinnamon.
- New York's state muffin is the apple muffin, yet again there were no specific designations as to when said muffin should be eaten.
- Pennsylvania also adopted the chocolate chip cookie as the commonwealth's official cookie, not making any claim for the cookie's origin (thank goodness).
- South Dakota's state dessert is kuchen, a German fruit- or cheese-filled yeast cake.
- Vermont's state pie is apple pie. Enough said.

No-Ice-Cream Chocolate Banana Sundae

Your dorm fridge probably doesn't have a freezer compartment, or if it does, isn't big enough to hold even a pint of ice cream. We came up with this dessert so that you can have the satisfaction of creating a sundae right in your own room.

Equipment Needed: electric grill, knife, plate, spatula

Preparation Time: 10 minutes

Ingredients:

> 1 banana, peeled and cut in half lengthwise
> 1 milk chocolate candy bar, broken into ½-inch squares
> 1 can whipped cream
> 1 handful raisins
> 1 handful nuts

Preparation:

1. Preheat electric grill as directed.
2. With the flat side of the sliced banana facing down, slice shallow pockets into the fruit without cutting through. You might have better luck starting with bananas that have been in your fridge for at least 10 minutes.
3. Insert the chocolate pieces into the banana pockets.
4. Carefully place the banana on the grill flat side down for 2 minutes or until the chocolate is melted.
5. Transfer the banana to a plate and cover with whipped cream, raisins, and nuts.

Servings: 1

Perfectly Healthy Dessert

You won't have to feel guilty about eating this treat all the time. It's a quick, sweet fix that's good for you.

Equipment Needed: plate or paper towel, spoon

Preparation Time: 1 minute

Ingredients:

> 1 graham cracker
> 1 tablespoon cottage cheese
> 1 teaspoon raisins
> 1 pinch of cinnamon
> ½ teaspoon honey (⅓ takeout packet)

Preparation: Place graham cracker on a plate (or a paper towel, napkin, or any other clean surface). Top with cottage cheese and spread gently. Cover with the raisins, cinnamon, and the honey.

Servings: 1

Chocolate Is Good Enough to Eat

To many, dessert signifies the end of a good meal. Others like to finish eating with a sweet taste in their mouths. But according to *Psychology Today*, desserts, especially chocolate ones, may be one of the most important parts of the meal. Chocolate turns out to be a good source of antioxidants—the chemicals known for their cell-protecting properties. Antioxidants fight off free radicals, the wildly reactive oxygen molecules that damage our cell membranes and DNA. Free radicals are thought to promote heart disease by oxidizing the "bad" (LDL) cholesterol, leading to hardened arteries, and are also linked to cancer and other degenerative diseases affecting all parts of the body.

The body gets the benefits of antioxidants both by manufacturing them and consuming them in foods. All plants have at least a small amount of antioxidants, and some produce large quantities, including berries, dark teas, garlic, and red wine. But a chemistry professor at the University of Scranton, in Pennsylvania, says that cocoa beans top them all. Dr. Joe Vinson's research has shown that cocoa beans are the most potent source of polyphenols, a type of antioxidant. Dark chocolate has twice as much as milk chocolate, but white chocolate has no antioxidants at all.

So think of chocolate as a health food, and don't sweat the waistline ramifications if you indulge in a little bit every day. Overall, you're doing the rest of your body a favor by feeding your sweet tooth!

Not-Quite-Baked Apple

Equipment Needed: microwave oven, knife, two microwavable bowls or cups, paper towel

Preparation Time: 5 minutes

Ingredients:

1 teaspoon sugar (1 takeout packet)
1 pinch of cinnamon
1 teaspoon butter (½ pat)
1 green apple, such as Granny Smith, sliced in half, core removed
1 dollop whipped cream

Preparation:

1. Mix the sugar and cinnamon into the butter in a small bowl or cup. Set aside.
2. Set the apple in a small bowl. Fill the core area with butter mixture and pat firmly into the center of the fruit.
3. Cover the apple bowl with a paper towel. Microwave on HIGH for 2 to 3 minutes, or until the apple is tender. Top with whipped cream.

Servings: 1

> **In Case You Mess Up**
>
> If you have overcooked a baked apple and it becomes mushy, don't throw it out. Add another 2 teaspoons of sugar and cook for another minute. After the mixture cools, put in the fridge and have it as breakfast jam on a slice of bread!

Dried Fruit Balls in a Graham Cracker Crust

Equipment Needed: knife, cutting board, bowl

Preparation Time: 15 minutes, plus 15 minutes chilling

Ingredients:

½ pound dried apricots and papaya, chopped
½ cup brown sugar
½ cup walnuts, chopped
½ (14-ounce) can
1 cup finely crushed graham crackers

Preparation:

1. Place the dried fruit in a bowl and toss with brown sugar. Stir in the walnuts and condensed milk.
2. Refrigerate the mixture for at least 15 minutes. When you are ready to serve, shape the mixture into 1-inch balls and roll in crushed graham crackers.

Servings: 10

Go-Crazy Swap:

Substitute any dried fruits that you like, including raisins, dried cranberries, or dried cherries, as long as they measure ½ pound in total.

Chocolate-Dipped Strawberries

Equipment Needed: microwave oven, microwavable bowl, toothpicks, parchment or waxed paper

Preparation Time: 15 to 20 minutes (depending on whether chocolate needs to be reheated), plus 15 minutes to set chocolate

Ingredients:

3 ounces or 6 squares semisweet or bittersweet chocolate, chopped
16 strawberries, washed and dried, but not trimmed (make sure to choose firm, red strawberries without any soft spots)

Preparation:

1. Place the chocolate into a microwavable bowl. Microwave at MEDIUM power for 1 minute or until the chocolate melts (stirring after 30 seconds). Be careful not to overheat the chocolate!

2. Place one toothpick halfway into the stem of each straw-
    berry, then lay strawberry on the parchment paper.
3. Dip each strawberry into the melted chocolate, allowing the
    excess to drip off. Place the dipped strawberry back on the
    parchment paper. If the chocolate becomes hardened, you
    may want to microwave it again for 15 seconds at MEDIUM
    power.
4. Refrigerate for approximately 15 minutes, until the choco-
    late sets. Keep these in the refrigerator if you are not eating
    them immediately. If not properly stored, they will become
    very soggy.

Servings: 4

Go-Crazy Swap:

A great variation of this recipe is to use white chocolate. Buy both
and experiment. Or, swap out the strawberries for a different fresh
or dried fruit. You can try pineapple slices, apple, or dried apricots,
pears, or mango.

Most Creative Crispy Rice Treats

Your favorite after-school snack does not have to be discarded once
you are in college. These treats can become a conversation piece for
almost any occasion if you have a few additional ingredients.

Equipment Needed: microwave oven, baking sheet, waxed paper,
parchment paper, microwavable plastic wrap, spoon, microwavable
bowl

Preparation Time: 15 minutes

Basic Ingredients:

> ¼ cup butter (6 pats)
> 10 ounces marshmallows
> 6 cups crispy rice cereal

Preparation:

1. Put butter and marshmallows in a microwavable bowl and microwave the mixture on HIGH for 2 minutes. Stir to combine.
2. Microwave on full power 1½ to 2 minutes longer, or until the mixture is melted. Stir until smooth.
3. Add the cereal and stir until it is well coated.
4. Using your hands or waxed paper, press the mixture evenly into a baking sheet covered with parchment paper. Place in refrigerator until cool. Cut into 2-inch squares, or as big as you desire. To keep leftovers fresh, immediately wrap each individual square in plastic wrap, and refrigerate until needed.

Servings: 35-40 pieces

Choose from the following selections to improve upon this classic dessert:

Go-Crazy Swap:

Let's say you really crave this snack, but you don't have the right cereal on hand. Try the same recipe with a whole new cereal. Anything crunchy will do: go back to your cereal matrix and swap!

OCCASIONS	INGREDIENTS ADDED DURING STEP 3
Valentine's Day	1 cup cranberries or any red button candies
St. Patrick's Day	1 cup green chocolate chips or green sprinkles
Halloween	1 cup Halloween "corn" candies
Any other special day (birthdays, second dates, flunking Statistics, etc.)	1 cup of any one of the following: • M&Ms • chocolate chips • raisins • crystallized ginger

Banana Cream Pudding

Equipment Needed: large mixing bowl, four serving bowls, spoon

Preparation Time: 10 minutes, plus 20 minutes for chilling

Ingredients:

> 2 tablespoons instant banana pudding mix
> 2 tablespoons instant vanilla pudding mix
> 2 ½ cups whole milk
> 2 cups (1 pint) whipped cream or whipped topping
> 2 cups round vanilla wafers

Preparation:
1. Mix the pudding mixes together in a large bowl.
2. Add the milk, mix until smooth, and fold in the whipped cream.
3. Line four serving bowls with the vanilla wafers. Pour the mixture on top, and refrigerate for 20 minutes before serving. If there is leftover pudding, keep refrigerated for second helpings!

Servings: 4

More-Than-Just-Fruit Dessert

Equipment Needed: bowl, spoon

Preparation Time: 5 minutes

Ingredients:

>   3 tablespoons sour cream
>   1 teaspoon sugar (1 takeout packet)
>   1 peach or plum
>   1 cup any berries (strawberries, blueberries, raspberries, blackberries)
>   1 cookie, any variety

Preparation:

1. In a bowl, mix together the sour cream and sugar.
2. Cut the peach into bite-size slices and add to the bowl. Add the berries and gently mix.
3. Crumble the cookie on top and enjoy.

Servings: 1

College Milk Shake

We discovered this recipe because we were throwing a party and bought a ton of ice cream and forgot we didn't have a freezer. Fortunately for us, someone was brewing a pot of coffee, and we were inspired!

Equipment Needed: coffeemaker (optional), blender

Preparation Time: 2 minutes

Ingredients:

> 1 cup coffee, bought or prepared as you prefer
> 1 scoop vanilla ice cream
> 1 pinch of cinnamon

Preparation:

1. Pour the coffee into the blender.
2. Add the ice cream and blend until smooth. Pour into a serving glass and top with cinnamon.

Servings: 1

Microwave S'mores

Equipment Needed: microwave oven, microwavable plate, paper towel

Preparation Time: 2 minutes

Ingredients:

> 2 large graham crackers
> 1 milk chocolate candy bar
> 2 marshmallows

Preparation:

1. Place ½ graham cracker on the microwavable plate. Top it with ¼ chocolate bar and marshmallow. Cover with remaining half graham cracker, and cover with a paper towel.
2. Heat on HIGH for 1 minute or until the whole thing melts. Let stand a minute before eating. Repeat with the remaining ingredients, if you haven't eaten them already.

Servings: 1

A Summer of S'mores

The s'more is a Girl Scout tradition that started back in the 1920s. S'mores got their name from frequent requests for "some more" whenever they were made. You can celebrate this summer spectacular all year round with your microwave oven. But keep these dates in mind when you are indulging on a perfect s'more:

July 7: Chocolate Day
August 10: National S'mores Day
August 30: National Toasted Marshmallow Day

BEVERAGES

When the publisher asked us to write a cookbook for college students, they wanted a chapter on drinks. We smiled, naturally! Unfortunately, you will not get a glimpse of our bartending wizardry. The publishers insisted that this book contain no references to alcohol. So what you have here are great, thirst-quenching ideas for hot and cold days, for yourself or for parties. Enjoy!

Fancy Hot Apple Cider

Equipment Needed: microwave oven, pitcher, microwavable mug, spoon

Preparation Time: 5 minutes

Ingredients:

> ½ cup orange juice
> 4 cups pasteurized apple cider (found in the refrigerated section of the supermarket)
> 1 tablespoon crystallized ginger*
> 2 teaspoons ground cinnamon
> 4 teaspoons sugar, or 4 takeout packets

*If you cannot find crystallized ginger, you can substitute a few peeled slivers of fresh ginger, or, if all else fails, just omit it.

Preparation:

1. Pour the orange juice, apple cider, and ginger into a pitcher. Pour directly into four mugs. Microwave each cup on HIGH for 1 minute without boiling.
2. Sprinkle ½ teaspoon cinnamon and 1 teaspoon sugar over each mug.

Servings: 4

Crystallized Ginger

Crystallized ginger is ginger root that has been cooked in sugar syrup and further coated with sugar, turning an ordinary root vegetable into a piece of candy. With a strong spicy taste, crystallized ginger is a real palate cleanser. When used in the recipe above, it also works as a "dessert to a dessert": once the cup of hot cider is finished, the remaining ginger pieces can be eaten like the candy it truly is.

Thai Coffee

We first tried Thai coffee in a small basement restaurant in New York's Chinatown. A few years later, we tasted a similar drink, and notwithstanding inflation, the same $1 drink became a $4 smoothie in a coffee chain that may not be too far from your campus. The good news is that this drink is much easier to make than you think! The only question is whether or not you are patient enough to wait until it chills.

Equipment Needed: microwave oven, microwavable mug, can opener, spoon

Preparation Time: 6 minutes, plus 5 minutes to chill

Ingredients:

> 2 teaspoons instant coffee crystals*
> 8 ounces water
> 2 tablespoons sweetened condensed milk

* Thai coffee is served very strong, and this recipe calls for a stronger brew than you may be used to. You may need to adjust the amount of coffee to your taste.

Preparation:

1. Add coffee crystals to water and heat in microwave on HIGH for 1 minute without boiling.
2. Add 2 tablespoons of condensed milk. Chill the mug in the refrigerator for 5 minutes.

Servings: 1

> **The Joys of Condensed Milk**
>
> If you are a person who loves to eat ice cream out of a container, we may have just introduced you to an even worse indulgence. Although typically we tell you what to do with the leftovers, we are not too worried about what will happen to an opened can of sweetened condensed milk. Prepared by boiling down a mixture of whole milk and sugar until 60 percent of the water evaporates, this concoction has been called "dessert magic" by chefs and home cooks alike. Try to use it as called for in the recipes throughout this book, and keep your spoons safely tucked away whenever you open a can.

Lemon and Cucumber Water

We would never have stumbled upon this drink had it not been for one of our dorm mates, whose mother owns a famous spa in California. When she came to visit, she made it for us. Although we do not think this is a very manly drink, it is very refreshing. More importantly, all of the ladies love it!

Equipment Needed: pitcher (or a large jar), vegetable peeler, spoon

Preparation Time: 5 minutes

Ingredients:

> ½ cucumber
> 6 cups water
> 3 tablespoons lemon juice

Preparation:

1. Cut the cucumber lengthwise and run a spoon down the middle, removing the seeds. Peel and discard the skin, and cut the cucumber into thin slices and put it into the pitcher.
2. Add water and lemon juice to the pitcher, and refrigerate for a few minutes before serving.

Servings: 6

Grandmother's Get-Well Tea

There are few lonelier moments than when you find yourself sick for the first time at college and realize that no one will be taking care of you. Drinking this tea will make you feel better. What's more bringing this tea to a sick friend may guarantee friendship for life (or at least until full recovery).

Equipment Needed: microwave oven, microwavable mug, spoon, knife, cutting board, saucer or small plate

Preparation Time: 7 minutes

Ingredients:

>   6 ounces water
>   1-inch piece fresh ginger, peeled and chopped
>   1 tablespoon honey (1½ takeout packets)

Preparation:

1. Boil water in the microwave oven on HIGH for 2 minutes.
2. Put ginger pieces and honey into the cup. Stir, cover, and let stand for 5 minutes.
3. If you do not like floating ginger pieces, you can strain them out before drinking.

Servings: 1

Chai Tea on a Budget

Equipment Needed: microwave oven, microwavable mug, spoon, stapler

Preparation Time: 5 minutes

Ingredients:

>   1 tea bag
>   ¼ teaspoon ground cardamom
>   1 pinch of saffron
>   8 ounces water
>   2 tablespoons sweetened condensed milk

Preparation:

1. Open the tea bag carefully at the top and add to it the cardamom and saffron. Staple the tea bag back together.
2. Put the water in a microwavable mug and heat on HIGH for 2 minutes or until it boils. Place the tea bag in the cup and let stand for 2 minutes (longer, if you like strong tea).
3. Add condensed milk and stir carefully.

NOTE: This recipe is excellent cold. You can brew the tea, mix it with condensed milk, and let stand until it cools.

Servings: 1

Refreshing Cranberry-Orange Drink

Equipment Needed: pitcher

Preparation Time: 1 minute

Ingredients:

>   1 cup cranberry juice cocktail
>   1 cup orange juice

Preparation: Mix all ingredients into a pitcher and pour into serving glasses.

Servings: 2

Punch without a Punch

Equipment Needed: microwave oven, microwavable bowl, large punch bowl, serving ladle, pitcher

Preparation Time: 5 minutes, plus 10 minutes to chill

Ingredients:

>   2 cups water
>   8 green tea bags
>   15 teaspoons sugar, or 15 takeout packets
>   ¼ cup lemon juice, or the juice from 1 lemon
>   6 cups grape juice
>   8 cups club soda

Preparation:

1. Put the water in a microwavable bowl and heat on HIGH for 2 minutes, or until it boils. Put tea bags into the water, and steep for 2 minutes.
2. Combine with the sugar, lemon juice, and grape juice in a pitcher and refrigerate for at least 10 minutes. When ready to serve, pour into a punch bowl and add the soda.

Servings: 16 to 20

Traditional Hot Chocolate Made Easy

Anyone can make instant hot chocolate with water, but it really tastes better, and more like hot chocolate is supposed to taste, if you spring for the milk and fresh marshmallows.

Equipment Needed: microwave oven, microwave-safe mug, spoon

Preparation Time: 3 minutes

Ingredients:

>   8 ounces milk
>   1 (1-serving envelope) any hot chocolate mix
>   2 large marshmallows
>   ¼ teaspoon ground cinnamon

Preparation:

1. Pour milk into a microwavable mug. Heat the milk on HIGH for 1½ minutes: you are not boiling the milk, just making it hot.
2. Stir in the hot cocoa mix. Drop in marshmallows and dust with cinnamon. Drink, and save the marshmallows for last!

Servings: 1

What Else Goes in Hot Drinks?

- Fruit syrups: If you have access to them, raspberry or cherry syrup is fantastic with hot chocolate, a bland tea, or strong coffee. Don't use more than 1 teaspoon, even if you like your drinks sweet. One bottle should last your entire college career.
- Grated chocolate: There's no such thing as too much chocolate. Adding chocolate to coffee sounds like a great idea, but is adding it to hot chocolate just plain redundant? No way! Just add a few slivers to the top of your cup, and the first thing that will hit you will be the aroma of real chocolate. If you have a grater and a dark chocolate bar, grate a few slivers on top of the finished drink. Or you can just eat the bar while you are preparing your beverage.

Almost-Homemade Lemonade

This lemonade recipe will turn out very sweet if you choose a mix that is loaded with sugar or sugar substitute. Try to find an instant brand that is on the tarter side. Play around with the choices of sugar substitutes; some of these actually taste sweeter than the ones that use traditional sugars.

Equipment Needed: pitcher larger enough to hold 6 cups of water, hot pot or microwave oven, and microwavable bowl (if you need to dissolve the lemonade mix in warm water)

Preparation Time: 2 minutes, 15 minutes to chill

Ingredients:

2 tablespoons honey (3 takeout packets)
4 to 8 cups hot water
1 (1-serving envelope or measure) powdered lemonade mix
1 lemon, sliced

Preparation:

1. Mix the honey into 2 tablespoons of hot water.
2. Prepare the lemonade mixture using the package recipe. Add the dissolved honey into the lemonade mixture and mix. Add lemon slices and refrigerate for at least 15 minutes before serving.

Servings: Depending on the mix, you may end up making at least 4 servings

Fresh Watermelon and Apple Drink

Equipment Needed: blender, knife, cutting board, vegetable peeler, strainer, pitcher

Preparation Time: 20 minutes, plus 15 minutes chilling

Ingredients:

4 Granny Smith apples, peeled and chopped
¼ cup lemon juice, or the juice of 1 lemon
1 medium-size watermelon
1 to 4 tablespoons honey (1½-6 takeout packets), depending on the sweetness of the watermelon

Preparation:

1. Place the apples and the lemon juice in a blender and liquefy. Transfer the liquid to a pitcher.

2. Cut watermelon in half, removing the meat from the rind. Cut into cubes; don't worry about the seeds. Place the watermelon in the blender and liquefy. Depending on the size of the watermelon, you may need to liquefy it in more than one batch.
3. Pour the juice through the strainer and into the pitcher of apple juice. Throw away the pits.
4. Taste; adjust the flavor by adding honey, 1 tablespoon at a time. Refrigerate for at least 15 minutes before serving.

Serving: 6+, depending on the size of the watermelon

The Importance of Water

All of the beverages in this chapter are tasty, refreshing, and fun to make. But more important than drinking any of these is to make sure that you get lots of water throughout the day. Most doctors recommend that you drink at least eight 8-ounce glasses of water each day to be optimally hydrated. Drinking lots of water makes you less sleepy and allows you to think more clearly, two key functions for any busy student. Drinking water is good for your appearance: it keeps your skin supple and your complexion clear. It also helps all aspects of your total body health. It doesn't have to be fancy bottled water, or "flavored," or part of an "energy drink." Just raise a glass you've drawn straight from your closest tap, and toast yourself to good health throughout the day.

HOLIDAY MEALS AND SPECIAL OCCASIONS

There may be times when you can't get home to your family for the holidays. Instead of feeling lonely, invite some friends over and create a new holiday tradition. These recipes may sound familiar, but they have been modified for your cooking lifestyle. They also serve as a complete menu plan if you want to cook an entire meal for someone special. Simply prepare one item from each course and two side dishes for a complete holiday or special-occasion meal.

First-Course Suggestions

Asparagus in Bacon Blankets

Equipment Needed: microwave oven, microwavable plate, paper towels, microwavable plastic wrap

Preparation Time: 10 minutes

Ingredients:

> 10 strips bacon, sliced in half crosswise
> 20 asparagus spears, washed and ends trimmed about 1 inch from bottom
> ¼ cup water

Preparation:

1. Lay the bacon on a microwavable plate lined with two paper towels and microwave on HIGH for 2 minutes. You are not fully cooking the bacon at this point: you want it to be brown but still flexible enough to wrap around the asparagus. Set aside.
2. Place the asparagus in a microwavable dish with the water. Cover tightly with microwavable plastic wrap. Microwave on HIGH for 3 minutes.
3. When both the bacon strips and the asparagus are sufficiently cooled, wrap each strip of bacon around an asparagus spear, leaving tip and end exposed.
4. Lay a clean piece of paper towel on the microwavable plate and place the asparagus with bacon on top. Microwave for another 2 minutes, or until the asparagus begins to soften and bacon strips are brown and crispy. If extra cooking time is needed, add in increments of 30 seconds.
5. Serve warm or at room temperature.

Servings: 4

Vegetable Spring Rolls

Equipment Needed: paper towel, plate

Preparation Time: 10 minutes

Ingredients:

      1 pound firm tofu
      1 head Boston lettuce, or another variety with large, soft leaves
      8 ounces any type sprouts (soybean, alfalfa, mung bean, etc.)
      ½ cup thinly sliced red or yellow bell peppers
      ½ cup of your favorite Asian-style salad dressing, such as a soy ginger or shiitake mushroom and sesame

Preparation:

1. Place the tofu on a plate and gently press it to remove any excess water. Cut the tofu horizontally into three sections and then vertically into four strips.
2. Cut four large lettuce leaves from the stem, wash them, and dry the leaves on a paper towel.
3. When dry, place a lettuce leaf on a plate. In the center of the lettuce, place a ¼ cup of sprouts. Top with a few pepper slices, 3 strips of tofu, and 2 tablespoons of salad dressing. Fold the outer leaves toward the center so that they cover each other, and then fold one of the ends over. Turn the packet upside down, and serve on a clean plate. Pick up and eat with your hands like an egg roll or a burrito.

Servings: 4

Appetizers Are Meant to Be Just That

Don't worry that these recipes deliver small portions. Appetizers are meant to prepare your palate and your stomach for the rest of the meal. They are purposefully small in size and served at the beginning of the meal to inspire the appetite. This way, you'll fully enjoy the rest of the dinner and have plenty of room for dessert.

Main-Course Suggestions

Juicy Microwave Turkey Breast

Equipment Needed: microwave oven, microwavable baking pan large enough to hold the turkey breast, waxed paper, sharp carving knife, instant-read thermometer, two cups, one with cover

Preparation Time: 40 minutes

Ingredients:

1 (3-pound) turkey breast (defrosted)
1 cup orange juice
4 tablespoons soy sauce, or 4 takeout packets
½ cup maple syrup

Preparation:

1. Put the turkey breast in a microwavable baking dish, skin down. Cover with waxed paper, and microwave on MEDIUM for 21 to 28 minutes, rotating the dish every 15 minutes. Since metal meat thermometers cannot be inserted in the turkey breast during microwave cooking; check doneness after 21 minutes by inserting an instant-read thermometer. A turkey

breast is done when the temperature in the thickest part reaches 170°F. If this temperature is not reached, put the turkey back in for the remaining 7 minutes, and check again. Repeat at 2-minute intervals if necessary.

2. Meanwhile, combine the orange juice and soy sauce in a covered cup and shake until fully incorporated. Set aside.

3. In another cup, dilute the maple syrup with 2 tablespoons of cooking liquid removed from the turkey pan. Baste the top of the turkey breast with the liquid and microwave on HIGH for 1 minute.

4. Remove the turkey from the microwave oven, and let stand for 5 minutes. Slice the turkey into ½-inch slices, working from the outside toward the bone, and pour the orange juice mixture over them.

Servings: 4 to 6

Grilled Lamb with Zucchini and Mushrooms

Lamb is always associated with special occasions and expensive meals. This recipe can be viewed as a complete meal, so no other side dishes are required.

Equipment Needed: electric grill, knife, cutting board, plate

Preparation Time: 20 minutes

Ingredients:

4 lamb chops (either shoulder or loin cuts)
4 tablespoons olive oil
¼ cup fresh cilantro, stems removed and leaves chopped
3 zucchini, peeled and sliced ¼-inch thick
8 mushrooms, any variety, sliced

Preparation:

1. Preheat electric grill as directed.
2. Coat the lamb with 1 tablespoon of oil on each side.
3. Place the lamb chops on the grill and cook for 5 minutes. You might wish to cook it longer if you like your lamb more well done, or if the chops are particularly thick. However, remember that lamb cooks very fast.
4. Transfer the lamb onto a serving plate. Sprinkle the chopped cilantro on top and drizzle 1 tablespoon of olive oil. Let stand for 5 minutes before serving.
5. Meanwhile, place sliced zucchini and mushrooms on the grill and cook for 3 to 5 minutes. If you prefer your veggies to have a fresh and crispy texture, use less time. If you you're your veggies very soft, cook longer.
6. Transfer the vegetables to the serving plate and drizzle the remaining olive oil on top.

Servings: 4

LEFTOVER IDEAS: After the meal, if you have any veggies left over, save them for the next day's omelet or lunchtime salad.

Spaghetti Squash with Cranberries and Almond

If you or your dining companion is a vegetarian, this recipe provides a very filling and beautiful entrée. You can serve this with any of the side dishes as well for a complete meal. The secret to vegetarian cooking is to create a colorful plate. That way, you are getting the most nutrition out of the meal.

Equipment Needed: microwave oven, microwavable plate and bowl, microwavable plastic wrap, sharp knife, fork

Preparation Time: 20 minutes

Ingredients:

> 2 cloves garlic, minced
> ½ cup minced fresh cilantro
> ½ cup sliced almonds
> 1 (3- to 4-pound) spaghetti squash
> 3 tablespoons olive oil

Preparation:

1. Combine garlic, cilantro, and almonds in a small bowl. Set aside.
2. Prick the squash four to five times with a small knife and put it on a microwavable plate. Cover with plastic wrap and microwave on HIGH for 10 minutes, or until the squash is soft to the touch. Allow the squash to stand covered for covered for 5 minutes. Take off plastic wrap, cut the squash in half lengthwise, and remove the seeds and gooey center.
3. Run a fork down the meat of the squash, separating the meat from the skin and into strands. The strands will look like orange spaghetti. Place the squash strands into a microwavable bowl. Gently toss with the garlic mixture. Microwave on MEDIUM for 2 minutes, or until all the ingredients are warm. Serve immediately.

Servings: 4 to 6

WHAT ELSE: Once you've mastered cooking spaghetti squash, it can be used as a replacement for pasta in almost any recipe. For example, top your squash with your favorite spaghetti sauce and sprinkle with Parmesan cheese for another complete meal.

Setting a Holiday Table

A holiday meal becomes special when you pay attention to the details, so that the holiday stands apart from every other meal you've eaten. First, make sure you have access to a table; rent a card table if you have none and pull up your desk chair(s) for a proper meal. Spring for a tablecloth to brighten the atmosphere: it can be cloth or a funky paper print from a party goods store. Set the table before you start cooking so that it will be ready for you and your guest(s) when you are ready to eat.

Lastly, make yourself a centerpiece. Buy one type of seasonally fresh fruit (pears, apples, peaches, depending on the season), and arrange them in a bowl with a handful of rinsed leaves from the great outdoors. Not only will it be pleasing to look at, you can help yourself to dessert when you're done!

Side Dish Suggestions

Two side dishes round out a perfect meal. One can be a simple green salad or a single microwaved vegetable. Choose from these others as a last complement.

Carrot and Daikon Salad

Equipment Needed: microwave oven, microwavable bowl, microwavable plastic wrap, knife, spoon

Preparation Time: 15 minutes

Ingredients:

2 cups baby carrots
2 cups daikon, cut into ½-inch cubes (see page 73 for more
about this Japanese root vegetable)
2 tablespoons water
½ cup honey (12 takeout packets)
2 tablespoons raisins
2 tablespoons butter (3 pats)

Preparation:

1. Combine carrots and daikon with the water in a microwav-
    able bowl. Cover with microwavable plastic wrap and
    microwave on HIGH power for 8 minutes, stirring halfway
    through. Microwave additional time at 1-minute intervals
    if necessary.
2. Remove dish from microwave and uncover. Stir honey,
    raisins, and butter into the warm vegetables. Let stand for 5
    minutes before serving.

Servings: 4

Mashed Potatoes

Even if there was time to mash potatoes by hand, it still makes more
sense to use a prepared mix. It's easy, fast, and by far the most delicious way to make them. Try these add-on suggestions to give these
spuds more zing.

Equipment Needed: Microwave oven, two microwavable bowls,
spoon

Preparation Time: 5 minutes

Ingredients:

1 cup mashed potato mix

Other ingredients typically called for preparing the mix include:

1½ cups water
½ cup milk
2 tablespoons butter or margarine (we recommend butter)

For more variety, add two of the following:

1 tablespoon parsley or cilantro
1 tablespoon grated Cheddar or Parmesan cheese
1 clove garlic, finely chopped
1 tablespoon bacon bits

Preparation:

1. Pour water and milk into a microwavable bowl and heat on HIGH for 4 minutes or until boiling.
2. Carefully mix in butter, and set aside.
3. Place the potato mix into a large bowl. Pour in the hot liquid into the bowl. Mix and add other ingredients.

Servings: 4

Classic American Green Bean Casserole

Equipment Needed: microwave oven, 1½ quart microwavable casserole dish, microwavable plastic wrap, wooden spoon

Preparation Time: 20 minutes

Ingredients:

1½ cups fried onions
1 (10-ounce) can condensed cream of mushroom soup
¾ cup milk
2 (14-ounce) cans whole green beans, drained
salt and pepper to taste

Preparation:

1. Set aside ¾ cup of fried onions. In a casserole dish, mix remaining ingredients. Cover dish with plastic wrap and cook in the microwave oven on HIGH for 10 minutes, stirring halfway through, until all the ingredients are heated.
2. Remove from microwave oven and uncover dish. Sprinkle remaining onions on top and return, uncovered, to the microwave oven. Microwave on MEDIUM for 2 minutes. Let stand for 5 minutes before serving.

Servings: 4 to 6

Microwaving Vegetables

Most fresh vegetables can be prepared easily in the microwave oven. Here's a list of foolproof veggies that round out any holiday meal and are easy to prepare. Except for whole potatoes, vegetables should be covered while cooking. When cooking vegetables in microwavable cookware that has a lid, use the lid. If you don't have a lid, cover bowl or plate with plastic wrap into which you have poked a few small holes to let the steam escape. And always check foods halfway through the cooking time. Stir, rearrange, and/or turn over to ensure even cooking.

- Potatoes, sweet potatoes: Place potato on a plate, poking a few small holes in the potato as it releases air as it cooks. Cover with a paper towel and microwave on HIGH for 4 minutes. Cook four potatoes or yams for 12 to 14 minutes, arranging them in a circle in the microwave oven, about 1 inch apart from one another.
- Spinach: Rinse spinach and place in microwavable container. Do not add additional water, and microwave on HIGH for 4 to 6 minutes or until completely wilted.
- Peas, green beans, or broccoli: Put in microwavable container with ¼ cup water per pound, cover, and microwave on HIGH for 8 to 10 minutes per pound. Vegetables should be crisp not soggy, and bright in color.

Dessert Suggestions

Delicious Microwave Chocolate Cake

The hardest part of making a cake is icing it well. That's why we love this recipe: the icing is already on the cake before you take it out of the microwave oven. Your guests would never know that this wasn't baked in a proper oven.

Equipment Needed: mixing bowl, microwave oven, microwavable tube pan, rubber spatula, spoon, paper towel

Preparation Time: 10 minutes

Ingredients:

>¼ cup plus 1 tablespoon vegetable oil
>1 (16-ounce) can prepared frosting in your favorite flavor (vanilla, chocolate, or even coconut)
>1 (18.25-ounce) box chocolate cake mix
>1 cup water
>3 eggs

Preparation:

1. Pour 1 tablespoon of the oil onto a paper towel. Wipe down the entire pan.
2. Spoon frosting into the bottom of a baking pan. Set aside.
3. In a large bowl, mix together cake mix, water, remaining oil, and eggs until batter is smooth and glossy.
4. Spoon cake mixture into the pan on top of the frosting. Let the cake settle for a few minutes before cooking. Then, microwave on HIGH for 12 minutes. You will know if the cake is ready by gently inserting a fork into the middle. If it comes up clean, the cake is ready. If it comes up wet, or with

batter stuck to it, continue to cook in 2-minute intervals until done.

5. Let the cake sit for 10 minutes. Then, cover the baking pan with a clean plate. Carefully turn over baking pan and let cake slip out. If you are having difficulty removing the cake, run a knife around the edges, and tap the top of the pan before shaking the cake out.

Servings: 8 to 10

Holiday Egg Nog

This holiday classic uses uncooked eggs as its base. Make sure the drink does not stand at room temperature for too long.

Equipment Needed: blender

Preparation Time: 10 minutes

Ingredients:

>   4 eggs
>   1 cup can sweetened condensed milk
>   2 teaspoons vanilla extract
>   3 cups milk
>   1 cup heavy cream

Preparation:

1. Beat the eggs in a blender until they are foamy. Pour in the rest of ingredients and blend for 30 seconds.
2. Remove glass attachment from blender and place in refrigerator until you are ready to serve.

Servings: 4

Egg Nog Variation

Another egg nog option is to buy a large container of vanilla ice cream and store it in your refrigerator. Once it is completely melted, pour into glasses and dust on a little nutmeg and serve.

OFF-CAMPUS COOKING

Think of this chapter as Cooking 2.0. Now that you've mastered the recipes in the rest of the book, you're ready for the next level. What's different about these recipes is that they require something truly unique: an oven. Don't be scared: you'll finally be able to experiment with traditional heating elements and odd-shaped foods that wouldn't fit on your electric grill and feel the pleasure of cleaning pots and pans. We're so proud of you!

Better than Mom's Pancakes

Equipment Needed: stovetop, frying pan, spatula, two mixing bowls, wooden spoon, serving spoon, whisk

Preparation Time: 15 minutes

Ingredients:

> 1 cup flour, preferably whole wheat
> 1 teaspoon baking powder
> 1 egg
> 1 cup milk
> 2 tablespoons butter (6 pats)

Preparation:

1. Mix the dry ingredients together. Set aside.
2. In a separate bowl, beat the egg into the milk. Pour the liquids into the dry ingredients and mix gradually until the batter is smooth.
3. Place frying pan on the stovetop over medium heat. Place 1 tablespoon of the butter in the pan and melt it to grease the pan.
4. Using the largest spoon you have, drop pancake batter onto the pan, separating the pancakes by at least one inch. When the pancakes start to form holes on the top, flip them over and cook an additional 2 minutes until fully cooked. Add more butter as necessary to the pan between batches.

For Added Flavor:

Serve with maple syrup or your favorite jam.

Servings: Your yield will depend on the size of the spoon you use. This recipe will make enough pancakes to please at least three people.

Making Perfect Pancakes

There are two secrets to making perfect pancakes. The first is to throw away the first batch. No matter how patient you are, the pan or griddle will not be hot enough the first time around, and the first batch will always seem to be a little chewy. As the pan gets hotter, the pancakes will get both lighter and crisper, and the cooking time will decrease. Keep adding a little bit of butter between batches. By the second or third round, you'll have the system down pat.

The second is to warm up the syrup, assuming you like syrup. Pour out the amount you plan on using into a microwavable bowl or cup and heat on MEDIUM for 1 minute. This will take the edge off of a cold bottle or warm a room-temperature bottle. This way, when the syrup is poured on the pancakes, it won't make the pancakes instantly cold.

Open-Faced Breakfast Sandwiches

Equipment Needed: oven, stovetop, baking sheet, frying pan, paper towels, plate, fork, spatula

Preparation Time: 25 minutes

Ingredients:

    1 pound ground sausage meat
    4 eggs, beaten
    1 can refrigerated biscuit dough
    1 cup grated cheese

Preparation:

1. Preheat the oven to 450°F.
2. Place the sausage in the frying pan. Cook over medium-high heat until it is completely browned. Remove from frying pan and drain on a plate covered with paper towels.
3. Using the same frying pan, heat beaten egg mixture through until eggs are completely cooked.
4. Meanwhile, roll out each biscuit until fairly thin. Place on baking sheet. Sprinkle ground sausage over biscuits. Top with grated cheese.
5. Bake for 5 to 10 minutes, or until biscuits are golden brown.
6. Remove from the oven and top with the cooked eggs.

Servings: 4 (two biscuits per person)

Go-Crazy Add-ons:

Top your breakfast with a dollop of your favorite tomato sauce or a few drops of hot sauce for an extra zing.

Lunchtime Spanish Potato Omelet

This is the quintessential lunch food: hot and fresh, and easy to make. The secret to this Spanish classic is to cook the potatoes slowly without browning them.

Equipment Needed: oven, stovetop, frying pan, spatula, paper towels, plate, mixing bowl, spoon, knife, cutting board

Preparation Time: 30 minutes

Ingredients:

1 cup plus 5 tablespoons olive oil
2 large potatoes, peeled and sliced ⅛-inch thick
1 large onion, chopped

6 eggs
Sour cream (optional)

Preparation:

1. Heat 1 cup of the oil in a large nonstick frying pan over medium heat. Arrange a single layer of potatoes in the pan. Add a layer of onions, and then continue adding potatoes and onions in alternate layers.

2. Reduce the heat to low, and cook approximately 10 to 12 minutes, lifting and turning the potatoes occasionally, until they are cooked through but not brown.

3. Remove the cooked potato mixture to a plate lined with paper towels, and let drain. Pour out the remaining oil, and wipe the pan clean.

4. In a large bowl, beat eggs. Carefully add the potato mixture, gently pressing down with the back of the spatula so it is completely covered with egg. Let the mixture stand for 10 minutes.

5. Heat 3 tablespoons of oil in the pan over moderate heat until the pan is very hot but not smoking (otherwise the eggs will stick). Add the potato mixture, spreading it evenly around the pan. Reduce the heat to low, shaking the pan often and running the spatula around the side and bottom to make sure the omelet is not sticking.

6. After 8 minutes, the omelet should be cooked three-quarters of the way through. The top is no longer liquid and the bottom is beginning to brown. Remove the omelet from the pan by placing a large plate over the pan and invert the omelet onto the plate.

7. Add the remaining 2 tablespoons of oil to the pan. Gently slide the omelet brown side up back into the pan, and cook for 5 minutes or until the underside is moderately browned. Transfer omelet to a large plate and let it set for a few minutes before serving. This dish can be served at room temperature, and leftovers can be reheated.

8. When ready to serve, cut into pie-shaped wedges and serve with a dollop of sour cream.

Servings: 4

Go-Crazy Swap:

Like any other omelet, this one can stand the addition of leftovers. Instead of the sour cream, swap in anything left in your fridge, including sausage, veggies (fresh or canned), or cheese. Add these items in once the omelet begins to set in Step 5.

Perfect Roasted Lemon Chicken

Equipment Needed: oven, roasting pan, paper towels, aluminum foil, serving plate, carving knife

Preparation Time: 10 minutes, plus cooking time of 1 hour

Ingredients:

> 1 whole chicken (about 3 pounds)
> Salt and pepper
> 3 tablespoons butter (8½ pats)
> 1 tablespoon dried oregano
> 2 lemons, halved

Preparation:

1. Preheat oven to 425°F.
2. Rinse chicken with water, inside and out, and pat dry with paper towels. Sprinkle the salt and pepper inside and outside the chicken.
3. Rub the outside of the chicken with the butter, and sprinkle on the oregano. Squeeze 2 lemon halves gently, and rub the juice inside the chicken. Leave the lemons inside the chicken cavity during cooking.

4. Place the chicken in a roasting pan, breast side facing up. Cover loosely with aluminum foil so that hot steam can escape and so the top of the chicken does not burn.

5. Roast for 35 minutes. Carefully remove the foil and squeeze the second lemon on top of the chicken. Continue baking until the juices run clear when the thigh is pierced (about another 25 minutes).

6. Transfer chicken to a serving platter and let stand for a few minutes before carving. If you need to keep the chicken warm, cover it very loosely with foil.

Servings: 4

Go-Crazy Swap:

Change the seasoning by replacing salt, pepper, and oregano with a tablespoon each of ground cinnamon and cumin.

How to Carve a Chicken in 3 Easy Steps

Step One: Let the chicken rest, breast side up, for at least 5 to 10 minutes before you start carving. This will allow for the meat to set and the juices to remain in the meat.

Step Two: Taking a sharp knife, cut through the skin that connects the leg and the breast and slice down, pulling the thigh away from the bird. Continue until you reach the joint and cut through it to separate the leg. On a separate cutting board, cut through the joint between the thigh and drumstick. Repeat on the other side with second leg.

Step Three: Run the knife down one side of the breastbone. Run the knife under the breast meat all the way to the wing, and remove in one piece. On the cutting board, separate the wing at the joint. Repeat on the other side of the breastbone for the second piece of breast meat. What will be left is the wishbone, which can be popped off with a clean horizontal cut.

Baked Ham

Equipment Needed: oven, baking pan, knife

Preparation Time: 10 minutes, plus 1 hour cooking time

Ingredients:

1 (3- to 4-pound) semi-boneless, precooked, precut ham
16 ounces (½ liter) cola
½ cup orange juice

Preparation:

1. Preheat the oven to 350°F.
2. Place the ham in shallow baking pan so that the cuts on the ham are horizontal to the pan. Score 1-inch diamonds shapes along the top and sides of the ham, about ½ inch deep.
3. Mix the cola and orange juice, and pour over the ham. There should be at least ¼ inch of liquid on the bottom of the pan.
4. Bake for 1 hour, basting the ham with pan liquids every 20 minutes.

Servings: 8

Risotto

Risotto is a wonderfully creamy Italian rice dish. When risotto is offered in a restaurant it is usually one of the more expensive items on a menu, so we assumed that risotto is extremely difficult to make. Not true! The price probably has to do with the fact that someone in the kitchen has to be paid just to stir the pot.

Equipment Needed: stovetop, two large pots, spoon

Preparation Time: 30 minutes

Ingredients:

1 tablespoon olive oil
1 cup arborio rice
½ cup cooking white wine
5 cups chicken stock
¼ cup Parmesan cheese, grated

Preparation:

1. Heat the stock in the second pot, and keep it at a low simmer.

2. Pour the olive oil into one of the pots and heat over medium heat. When the pot seems warm, add the rice and stir until the grains are coated with oil.
3. Add the cooking wine and stir constantly over medium heat until the wine is absorbed.
4. Add 1 cup stock to the rice, stirring until liquid is absorbed. Add the remaining liquid 1 cup at a time, constantly stirring the rice. The total cooking time should be about 20 minutes. When finished, the rice will create its own creamy sauce; add additional stock if a creamier texture is desired.
5. Remove from heat, stir in the cheese, and serve immediately.

Servings: 4

Go-Crazy Add-ons:
Risotto is like mac and cheese; you can add any leftovers you might have in your fridge to make this a heartier meal. If you are looking for extra ideas, you can add any of the following:

- 1 cup cocktail shrimp (add during the last 2 minutes of cooking)
- ½ cup canned peas (add during the last 5 minutes of cooking)
- 2 tablespoons chopped fresh cilantro (add when the dish is finished)

Almost-Southern Fried Chicken

Equipment Needed: frying pan, paper towels, fork, baking pan, large mixing bowl, two plates

Preparation Time: 20 minutes, plus 20 minutes marinating, plus 40 minutes cooking

Ingredients:

> 4 pounds chicken, cut up (roughly 8 pieces)
> 4 cups buttermilk
> 2 cups flour
> 1 tablespoon paprika
> ¾ cup vegetable oil

Preparation:

1. Place the chicken pieces in a baking pan. Pour the buttermilk over the chicken and cover. Place baking pan in the refrigerator for 10 minutes. Uncover, and turn the chicken over and chill for additional 10 minutes.
2. Combine the flour and paprika in a large mixing bowl.
3. Heat the oil in 12-inch skillet over medium-high heat. The oil needs to be at least 1½ inches deep.
4. While the oil is heating, take each piece of chicken and roll it in the flour mixture to coat, one piece at a time. Place the coated pieces on a plate.
5. Carefully place the chicken pieces in the skillet a few at a time so that they are not touching. It may take a few batches to fry the entire chicken. When a brown crust begins to form, turn the chicken over and cook on the other side.
6. After the crust forms on both sides of the chicken, reduce the heat to medium and cook for another 15 minutes. The thinner and smaller pieces like wings will be done first. The chicken is done when the juices run clear.
7. Put the finished pieces on a plate lined with two layers of paper towels to absorb the excess oil.

Servings: 4 to 6

Baked Brie

Equipment Needed: oven, nonstick baking sheet

Preparation Time: 10 minutes, plus 25 minutes cooking, plus 5 to 10 minutes cooling

Ingredients:

>1 (8-ounce) round Brie cheese
>1 tube refrigerated crescent dinner or breakfast croissant rolls
>1 tablespoon brown sugar
>1 tablespoon diced almonds or walnuts
>1 box your favorite crackers

Preparation:

1. Preheat oven to 350ΥF.
2. On a baking sheet, lay out the crescent rolls so they connect and form one round circle that is a bit larger than the round of Brie. Place the Brie on top.
3. Cover with the remaining crescent rolls, pinching and sealing the dough so that the top of the dish is uniform and it connects with the bottom rolls.
4. Sprinkle brown sugar and sliced nuts over the dough.
5. Bake for 25 minutes, until golden brown. Let cool for 5 to 10 minutes before serving. To serve, cut into the dough and place slices on the crackers.

Servings: 10

Restaurant-Quality Lasagne

Equipment Needed: oven, lasagne pan or deep baking dish, aluminum foil, large bowl, spatula

Preparation Time: 20 minutes, plus cooking time of 1 hour

Ingredients:

>   1 cup grated Parmesan cheese
>   2 cups grated mozzarella cheese
>   2 cups ricotta cheese
>   26 ounces tomato-based pasta sauce
>   12 no-boil lasagna noodles

Preparation:

1. Preheat oven to 375°F. Set aside 6 tablespoons Parmesan cheese and ½ cup mozzarella cheese.
2. In a large bowl incorporate the remaining Parmesan and mozzarella cheeses with the ricotta cheese.
3. Spread 1 cup of sauce in the lasagne pan. Arrange 3 noodles over the sauce.
4. Transfer one-third of the cheese mixture onto the noodles using the following method: take a tablespoon of cheese mixture at a time and drop it onto the noodles. Repeat this in different sections of the noodles. Once you have transferred one-third of the cheese mixture, gently spread the small amounts to make sure that the noodles are completely covered.
5. Cover with one-third of the remaining pasta sauce.
6. Repeat step 3 through 5 two more times so that at the end you have three layers of noodles, cheese, and sauce.
7. Cover the remaining sauce by sprinkling the extra mozzarella and Parmesan cheeses on top reserved in step 1.
8. Cover the dish with foil and bake for 40 minutes.

9. Carefully uncover. Increase oven temperature to 400°F. Bake for another 20 minutes, or until the noodles are tender, the sauce visibly bubbles, and the edges of lasagne are golden. Let stand for 15 minutes, then divide into 8 servings. Using a spatula, remove each serving from the baking dish.

Servings: 8

Why Aluminum Foil Can Be Your Best Friend

Aluminum foil really didn't play much of a role in your dorm room kitchen, mostly because you can't microwave with it. But now that you have access to an oven, it comes in very handy. First, in the same way that plastic wrap made for the perfect lid for microwave cooking, foil does the same duty in the oven. You can also packet-cook with it, a technique that works well particularly with fish or fresh vegetables. Here you put all the ingredients and seasonings inside a packet created with foil, and cook. Your meal inside the packet will cook faster and have a more intense flavor. And as you can imagine, clean up is a breeze: just throw out the packet when you're done. Lastly, foil withstands cold as well as heat, so leftovers can be wrapped—and reheated—in the same container.

Brazilian Sausage Stew

Equipment Needed: large pot, stovetop, knife

Preparation Time: 30 minutes

Ingredients:

1 (16-ounce) can black beans, rinsed and drained
1¼ cups water
2 medium-size bay leaves (buy a small jar in the spice section, it will last through college and your first marriage)
Salt and pepper
1 pound Polish smoked sausage
1 box (about 8 ounces) of your favorite white rice

Preparation:

1. Place the black beans in a large pot along with ¼ cup of the water. Add the bay leaves and simmer over medium-high heat for 10 minutes. Taste the beans; adjust the flavor with salt and pepper if they are too bland.
2. Meanwhile, slice sausage ½ inch thick
3. Add the sausage to the pot and cover with the beans. If there is not enough liquid to cover the meat, add more water, a ¼ cup at a time, until the meat and beans are completely covered.
4. Simmer on low heat for 10 to 15 minutes, or until the sausage is completely cooked through.
5. Meanwhile, prepare the rice per the instructions on the package. Make enough rice to cover your servings.

Servings: up to 4

This Stew Is Really Called Feijoada

Traditionally, this dish is served with the following:

• Fresh spinach
• Unflavored bread crumbs sprinkled on top
• Oranges, cut into 4 to 6 slices each

Oven-Roasted Sweet and Spicy Potatoes

Equipment Needed: oven, baking pan, aluminum foil, fork, knife

Preparation Time: 10 minutes, plus 45 minutes cooking time

Ingredients:

¼ cup water
6 medium-size sweet potatoes, peeled and cut into ½-inch-thick slices
¼ teaspoon chili powder
1 tablespoon ground cinnamon
¼ cup brown sugar
4 tablespoons butter (6 pats)

Preparation:

1. Preheat oven to 350ΥF.
2. Pour water into the baking dish and add the potato slices. Sprinkle with chili powder, cinnamon, and sugar. Cover the baking pan with aluminum foil and bake for 25 minutes.
3. Uncover the potatoes. If it's not in pat form already, cut the butter into thin slices and drop over the potatoes. Re-cover, and cook for an additional 15 minutes.
4. Uncover and test with a fork. The potatoes are done if a fork can easily pierce one.
5. Bake uncovered for another 5 minutes, or until slightly crispy.

Servings: 6

Steamed Fish with Chickpeas

Equipment Needed: stovetop, large pot

Preparation Time: 10 minutes, plus cooking time of 30 minutes

Ingredients:

> 1 cup can chickpeas
> 1½ cups spaghetti sauce
> ½ cup water
> 16 ounces thick, white fish, such as halibut or cod

Preparation:

1. Put the chickpeas and spaghetti sauce in a pot and simmer over medium-high heat for 15 minutes.
2. Remove half of the cooked chickpeas and ¾ cup of sauce from the pot. Set aside.
3. Pour the water into the pot of chickpeas. Place the fish into the pot over the chickpeas. Cut fish to fit into the pot if necessary. Cover the fish with the remaining chickpeas and tomato sauce.
4. Cover the pot with a lid or aluminum foil, and simmer for 10 to 15 minutes, or until the fish is done. You can tell the fish is done if it flakes easily with a fork.

Servings: 2 to 4

Fancy Pasta and Scallops

Equipment Needed: large pot, frying pan, stovetop, serving dish

Preparation Time: 15 minutes

Ingredients:

> 1 pound spaghetti
> 4 cloves garlic, peeled and chopped
> ½ cup butter*
> 1 pound scallops (bay or sea scallops, whatever is available)
> 3 teaspoons dried mint or basil

*This equals one whole stick, which would be about 12 pats of butter. That's way too many pats to walk away with at one time, so plan ahead.

Preparation:

1. Boil water and prepare pasta according to package instructions. Drain and set aside.
2. Meanwhile, lightly sauté garlic in butter over medium heat. Add the scallops and cook just until they are opaque, about 3 minutes for each side.
3. Pour the scallops and butter sauce over the pasta in a serving dish and sprinkle with the dried herbs. Mix and serve.

Servings: 4 to 6

Pasta with Ham and Peas

Equipment needed: stovetop, saucepan, serving dish

Preparation Time: 40 minutes

Ingredients:

     1 pound any hollow pasta shape, like penne or ziti
     3 tablespoons olive oil
     2 cups Alfredo sauce or any other white Italian cheese sauce
     1 cup frozen peas
     1 cup diced ham

Preparation:

1. Boil water and cook pasta according to package directions. Drain and transfer the pasta to a serving dish and toss with the olive oil.
2. In a saucepan, heat the sauce until it begins to simmer.
3. Add the frozen peas and ham, and cook for another 5 minutes.
4. Pour the sauce over the pasta, mix well, and serve.

Servings: 4

Homemade Ice Cream without an Ice-Cream Maker

This is your basic vanilla ice cream recipe, but once you master it, you can make any flavor you prefer.

Equipment needed: large coffee can with lid, 1-pound coffee can with lid, freezer

Preparation Time: 30 minutes

Ingredients:

     1 pint light cream
     ½ cup sugar (24 takeout packets)
     1 teaspoon vanilla extract
     6 to 7 cups crushed ice
     ¼ cup rock salt

Preparation:

1. In the smaller coffee can, combine the cream, sugar, and vanilla. Put the lid on tightly and set aside.
2. Make a thin layer of crushed ice on the bottom of the larger coffee can, and sprinkle it with 1 tablespoon of the rock salt. Place the small can inside the large can.
3. Fill the space between the two cans using 2 tablespoons rock salt for every cup of crushed ice. Seal the large can with its lid.
4. Shake the large can steadily, but not vigorously, for 10 to 15 minutes. Lift out smaller can and carefully remove lid.
5. Scrape down sides of the can and stir together. If the ice cream is still too soft, add more ice and salt to the large can, and continue to shake until firm. Or, place in the freezer for ½ hour until ice cream settles.

Servings: 5

Flan

Equipment Needed: oven, blender, kettle, small pot, 9-inch cake or glass pan, a baking pan with sides at least 1-inch high (an aluminum tray can work well), large plate, knife. The 9-inch cake pan must be able to fit inside the baking pan.

Preparation Time: 20 minutes, plus 55 to 60 minutes baking, plus 30 minutes chilling.

Ingredients:

1 cup sugar (48 takeout packets; again, plan ahead)
1 (14-ounce) can sweetened condensed milk
1 (8-ounce) package cream cheese, softened
3 eggs
1 tablespoon vanilla extract

Preparation:

1. Preheat oven to 350°F.
2. In a small pot, heat and stir the sugar over very low heat until it becomes caramelized, or melted. It should take on a light brown color and first become clumpy like wet sand before it turns to a liquid. Pour into a 9-inch cake pan and very carefully tilt the pan in all directions so that it covers all sides of the pan.
3. In a blender, combine the condensed milk, cream cheese, eggs, and vanilla. Blend until completely smooth. Pour the mixture over the cooled caramelized sugar in pan.
4. Meanwhile bring about 3 cups water to a boil.
5. Place the larger baking pan in the oven. Carefully put the pan filled with the flan mixture into the larger pan. Then, carefully pour the hot water into the outer pan to a depth of ½ inch. Make sure that the water does not get into the pan containing the flan.
6. Bake for 55 to 60 minutes. Check after 50 minutes: if a knife inserted into the middle comes up clean, the dessert is done. Remove carefully from oven so you don't spill the hot water in the outer pan.
7. Cool and place in fridge to chill. Invert onto a large plate. Cut into 12 servings, and put each on a separate plate.

Servings: 12 servings

Poached Pears

Equipment Needed: stovetop, large saucepan

Preparation Time: 20 minutes, plus 20 minutes cooking

Ingredients:

> 2 cups sugar (96 takeout packets; again, plan ahead)
> 1 cup white cooking wine
> 4 cups water
> 1 tablespoon ground cinnamon
> 2 tablespoons vanilla extract
> 4 firm pears, peeled, halved, and cored

Preparation:

1. In a large saucepan, heat and stir the sugar over very low heat until it becomes caramelized, or melted. It should take on a light brown color and first become clumpy like wet sand before it turns to a liquid.
2. Add wine, water, cinnamon, and vanilla to the caramelized sugar. Mix and add pears.
3. Simmer, covered, for about 15 minutes, or until the pears are just tender but not mushy.
4. Serve hot or cold.

Servings: 8 servings

ABOUT THE DVD

Cheap, Fast & Easy is a Rutgers University Television Network production, under-written by Chamberlain Bros., a member of Penguin Group (USA), Inc. The attached DVD was recorded at Rutgers, the State University of New Jersey, in May 2005.

Special thanks to:

Lisa Hope King	Ilya Livshits	Jason Jankowski
Jaimini Shah	Constance Schwab	Mehdi Doumi
Christopher Waters	Patrick Simon	Jon LaDeau
Steve Zmijewski	Patrick Stahl	Justin LaDeau
Carlo De Vito	Sarah Fehder	Eric Swiontkowski
Matthew Weismantel	Steve Lemma	Kevin Ragone
Ron Martirano	Scott Miller	Rae Frisch
Alex Fahan	Corinne Conte	Cheryl Walker
Katie Dickson	Tiffany Burke	Sherri Somers
Ryan Monigan	Sharon Fan	Beckman Rich
Casey Waltz	Danielle Gallagher	Marybeth Schmutz
Randolph Pierce	Nicole DiStefano	

All post-production work was handled by
Corinne Conte and Chris Lackner.
©2005 Rutgers University

143